SIZING
PEOPLE UP

SIZING PEOPLE UP

A VETERAN FBI AGENT'S USER MANUAL FOR BEHAVIOR PREDICTION

ROBIN DREEKE
AND **CAMERON STAUTH**

PORTFOLIO / PENGUIN

Portfolio/Penguin
An imprint of Penguin Random House LLC
penguinrandomhouse.com

Most Portfolio books are available at a discount when purchased in quantity for sales
promotions or corporate use. Special editions, which include personalized covers, excerpts,
and corporate imprints, can be created when purchased in large quantities. For more information,
please call (212) 572-2232 or e-mail specialmarkets@penguinrandomhouse.com. Your local
bookstore can also assist with discounted bulk purchases using the Penguin Random
House corporate Business-to-Business program. For assistance in locating a
participating retailer, e-mail B2B@penguinrandomhouse.com.

Library of Congress Cataloging-in-Publication Data
Names: Dreeke, Robin, author. | Stauth, Cameron, author.
Title: Sizing people up : a veteran FBI agent's user manual for behavior
prediction / Robin Dreeke and Cameron Stauth.
Description: 1st Edition. | New York : Portfolio, 2020. | Includes index. |
Identifiers: LCCN 2019037863 (print) | LCCN 2019037864 (ebook) |
ISBN 9780525540434 (hardcover) | ISBN 9780525540441 (ebook)
Subjects: LCSH: Prediction (Psychology) | Behavioral assessment. | Trust.
Classification: LCC BF761 .D74 2020 (print) |
LCC BF761 (ebook) | DDC 155.2/8—dc23
LC record available at https://lccn.loc.gov/2019037863
LC ebook record available at https://lccn.loc.gov/2019037864

Printed in Canada
1   3   5   7   9   10   8   6   4   2

BOOK DESIGN BY LUCIA BERNARD

Penguin is committed to publishing works of quality and integrity.
In that spirit, we are proud to offer this book to our readers; however,
the story, the experiences, and the words are the author's alone.

Some of the events and anecdotes in the work are factual, such as 9/11 and the
Robert Hanssen case, but are derived from open sources and not from FBI investigations
or analysis. The stories, cases, and examples used throughout thereafter are based
on the career of the author but are fictional, including names and locations. The
methodologies of behavioral analysis and the recruitment of human sources are the tools and
techniques of the author, and not endorsed, taught, and/or acknowledged by the FBI.

For Our Families

Kim, Katelyn, and Kevin
and
Lori, Gabriel, and Adrienne

CONTENTS

PART I

FRIEND OR FOE?

1

PREVAIL IN A WORLD OF STRANGERS

September 11, 2001
FBI New York Field Office

It was a bluebird day, and the last moment of American innocence. Living was easy, money was flowing, democracy was flowering, the Cold War was over, and the United States was luxuriating in a new type of peace on earth: one that felt—as hard as it is to comprehend today—lasting.

Each day transitioned into the next so peacefully and predictably that the era's conceit was that we'd finally arrived at "the end of history"—in a good way, believe it or not.

The first shaky baby-steps to the new world order had been taken in 1982, when Ronald Reagan had finally agreed with the Soviet Union to freeze construction of all new nuclear weapons, by invoking the old Russian motto of *Doveryai no Proveryai,* meaning: "Trust, but verify." He meant that he'd only trust the Russians if they could prove they deserved it, with facts and figures.

Looking back, it might seem easy to predict that Soviet Russia would soon disband, but at that time their politics were almost completely unpredictable. Americans in both parties thought Reagan's deal was doomed. The left believed that trust based on verification wasn't trust at all, and the right thought that there was no such thing as trusting an enemy. They were both wrong. It worked, and I've never forgotten the lesson.

But that era was about to end. Trust, and the predictability that almost always accompanies it, would be over in a few seconds.

A colleague and I were standing in front of a food cart in the Wall Street district, just outside our towering regional HQ. It was eight forty-five in the morning, but I was ready for my second round of coffee, because I'd come to work at five a.m., excited just to be there at such a great time in the long American experiment of *trusting only the leaders who act in our own personal best interests:* a political philosophy that we call democracy.

I heard a thud.

It looked like a small plane had crashed into the North Tower of the World Trade Center. My colleague said, "Poor guy must have had a heart attack."

"At least it's not terrorism," I said.

We rushed back up to our offices, where almost everyone was standing at the windows, transfixed.

A fire truck from a station below screamed toward the scene, and it felt as if we had front-row seats to an inspiring display of heroism that would carry the country to even greater heights.

But five of the firefighters that I saw in the truck would soon be dead, along with hundreds of others.

Debris started to fall from the tower. But as it fell, I realized with a sick feeling that it was people, because their arms and legs were flailing.

Soon a fireball shot through the South Tower. I yelled, "Oh my God—it's terrorism!" and looked behind me. The room was empty.

Ten agents soon returned, all of them former marines, like me, and somebody said that truck bombs were headed for our building, which was one of the tallest in the neighborhood, and also a federal outpost.

"We gotta evacuate!" I shouted. I was a relatively new recruit at the

New York City field office, in a room filled with senior agents, but this was not the time for concern about overstepping authority.

"No!" one of the agents cried. "If it's your time to go, it's your time to go!"

I'd long considered that agent to be remarkably reasonable, but his emotion-driven exhortation was reckless and foolhardy. So I shot it down and helped organize a group that ran to an FBI command post at the base of the towers.

In an act of incredible courage, someone charged toward the towers to help one of the people who'd stumbled out of the building, but the rescuer got so close that he was killed by one of the jumpers. People were dodging falling debris and flailing people, but in the smoke and dust most people were invisible or looked like stick figures.

Men and women were risking their lives for strangers, but many people—understandably—cowered in fear or just disappeared. Some were dumbstruck, but others operated with the military precision of soldiers in combat.

An agent I'd worked with, Lenny Hatton—an ex-marine explosives specialist who'd worked three prior terrorist attacks, and had just testified in an al-Qaeda trial—recognized the need for a communications network from inside the towers. So he ran into the darkness as everyone else was running out.

It was possible, but unlikely, that Lenny had made contact with my former boss at the FBI, John O'Neill, who was on his first day as the head of security at the World Trade Center. John and his team had solved the 1993 bombing of the WTC, and he'd spent his last four years at the Bureau working the Osama bin Laden case, trying to convince people that bin Laden was capable of a direct hit on the U.S. At that moment, John was on the forty-ninth floor of the South Tower, commanding the evacuation and refusing to leave.

In the chaos, I was surrounded by agents I thought I knew well, but suddenly it seemed impossible to predict what any of them would do. Run? Hide? Help? Or go home to their families, instead of working

Ground Zero? As usual, there was no right or wrong—just reality. But being able to read the realities of the people around me was critically important, and in these desperate moments *I couldn't do it.* I thought I knew these people, but I realized that I knew only what they wanted me to know, due to their own modesty, secrecy, shame, subterfuge, or simple privacy. I was almost equally ignorant of their many virtues, including the raw physical courage of John and Lenny.

Everything had changed, and nothing was predictable.

I headed back to our tower, which seemed to be free from damage, although the third building destroyed that day had yet to fall. A few guys followed me, and I said, "Buddy up! It'll be worse if we have to die alone." One of our agents dropped back, then fell out.

The building started to tremble and sway, and everyone looked stricken. But it was caused by the first tower collapsing. When the second tower went down, we abruptly lost communications with Lenny.

He was dead. His last known words—spoken to a guy he'd saved, who was blinded and choking from the heat and filth—were, "I'm going back into the building." Lenny probably had no illusions about his odds of surviving. I thought I knew him well, but I'd had no idea that he was capable of compassion so deep that it overrode his terror.

John went down with that tower, too, after saving many lives. He lies now in a New Jersey grave commemorated with a small American flag. In 2002, PBS ran a *Frontline* episode about him—called "The Man Who Knew"—but I've never been able to watch it.

More than two hundred law enforcement officers from dozens of agencies joined the 338 firefighters who died not only as patriots, but as people so benevolent and brave that they made no distinction that day between friends and strangers.

That night, I found my car where I'd parked it, now with a jet engine in front of it. As I crept home through the wreckage, I traded stares with unblinking pedestrians and wondered who was waiting for someone they'd never again see. One of them, a woman standing by the curb, had obviously been crying, but handed me a bottle of water and said, "God bless." I was unable to even say thanks, but bowed my head.

I was face-to-face with the worst of times, and the best of people: a tragically common nexus. As always, the sudden and unexpected pain of that day carried an equally common and terribly bittersweet wisdom that simply said, "*Open your eyes, and see people the way they really are.*"

Even on this first day of the strange new America, the people I passed on the streets appeared to be struggling viscerally with that sudden challenge, applying the same stoic will to it that they applied to enduring the poisoned air and stench of death. Many looked numb, still locked in shock, and unable to see the new reality.

I didn't have that option. My profession, and my peers, were tasked by default with seeing past our pain, remaining rational, and delivering a *safe and sane* new worldview to the people on these streets, and far beyond.

I knew how hard it would be. Most people want to cast off their illusions—but who among us wants to be disillusioned?

Our intel strongly suggested that bin Laden was responsible, but it felt very much as if we didn't even need the intel—because virtually all of us had a gut feeling that it was him. I had a great deal of confidence in gut feelings back then. Now I don't.

My brain swarmed with a tangle of questions. Why hadn't the State Department or any of its three-letter agencies acted decisively on John's knowledge about bin Laden? What was next? Who was still in New York that we needed to worry about? *What can I do?*

And why had I been so utterly unable to know what my own closest colleagues would do when it mattered most? I felt very close to those people and had thought we were all connected, or were at least on the same wavelength. As an agent, I was supposed to have veritable X-ray vision, and if I couldn't predict my good friends' actions, how in God's name could I ever predict what the bad guys would do?

I had no answer. Obviously. But I promised myself I would find one. Growth also happens fast on the worst days.

It would have been nice, of course, to think I would do that for Lenny, who had four kids, and John, who had two. But it was too late for that.

Sizing People Up

Few of the most serious problems in life are as common as not being able to read people and accurately predict what they'll do. It's not because we're all loose cannons, compulsive liars, or have rapidly shifting personalities. It's because most of us hide or disguise the parts of our lives that we don't want others to see—particularly if there's something important at stake, like love, money, our careers, or our reputations.

Even good people feel the need to hide things, because nobody's perfect and everybody's vulnerable. A high percentage of people break rules and lie when they're desperate: for something they want or something they fear. But even people in comfortable situations often shade the truth and cut corners just to get a little further ahead in life.

Decent, moral people also shade the truth, because each of us wants to be loved, and sometimes we're afraid that our true selves aren't worthy of it.

Millions of people, though, conceal their agendas and hide the whole truth for reasons that are far darker—such as greed, manipulation, power, control, and deception. Sadly, that's very common, especially in difficult environments and situations. It's particularly likely when people rise to positions of power, even if it's a petty form of power.

Because people are so often unethical, when you're involved in something important with someone, and don't know what they'll do next, life can feel not only strange and disorienting, but frightening.

To soften this fickle and debilitating aspect of human nature, almost all societies attempt to create fair and binding methods of ensuring commitments, such as business agreements, prenuptials, religious rules, laws, manners, promises, and unspoken social contracts. Even so, most of us are still wary of other people from time to time, because we've all witnessed the destruction of airtight deals, friendships, marriages, alliances, romances, manners, laws, and child custody.

And at one time or another, we've all been cheated and lied to.

Sometimes sizing people up can feel almost impossible, especially in business deals, because you're often dealing with people you don't know well, in a very competitive environment, in which sharing is not the norm.

Even worse for most people, though, are the times when they can't even predict what their own friends and family will do. Divorces, domestic violence, suicides, custody battles, and sexually transmitted diseases—to name but a few—commonly come as great and terrible surprises. All these situations can cause hardship. When someone leads you astray in your profession, you can be crippled financially. And when a loved one betrays you, it can change your whole outlook on life.

These inevitable violations of our most sacred codes chip away at our highest values—including the one that influences, and often completely governs, most human transactions, from business deals to love itself. That lofty value is *trust*. Trust is the active form of faith. It demonstrates—in real time and in the real world—a belief that people will not only try to do what they say they will, but also have the competence and diligence to make it happen. A betrayal of trust is one of the most devastating experiences that can happen to any human being, partly because it's almost impossible *not* to take it personally. It wounds you deeper than an accidental loss, because it makes you not only doubt other people, but even yourself, thinking that you should have known better.

In this book, I'm going to show you how to know better.

It's not as hard as you might think. You do it by learning to predict what people will do in the most important situations, and why. When you know that, you can finally feel safer from further harm. Your heart will begin to heal from past experiences and your confidence will soar. With any luck at all, during the times it matters most, you won't get fooled again.

My education in this issue didn't come naturally or intuitively to me, partly because I'm a fairly typical type-A American male who has no innate gift for deciphering human behavior. Like so many others, I learned to analyze behavior the hard way—through trial and error—

before it dawned on me that I could create a system for understanding people: one that can be taught and refined, through fairly simple training.

Without this training, though, you'll probably still struggle to predict what people will do during critical, life-changing events. As always, the villains will manipulate, the variables will mount, and your mind will cloud with indecision and doubt—because when you don't know what to expect from people, it becomes almost impossible to make the careful plans that a successful life demands.

As the clock ticks, your doubt will deepen, and the dread of the decision will spread like a contagion and create problems all its own: the alienation of innocent people, the need to snoop into people's private lives, or the postponement of a decision until it's too late for due diligence. At that point, time runs out, and most people just cross their fingers, go with their gut, and roll the dice.

Unfortunately, people who lack all the facts make the correct decision only about half the time, according to the best studies in behavioral science. As a rule, it's not their fault, because the person they were trying to size up often manipulates the situation. Sometimes people mislead you without even knowing that they're doing it, because everybody likes to see themselves in the best possible light, so they often lie to themselves, and then spread the lie around. Such grandiose myths often become part of a person's basic reputation. How often have you met somebody who's supposed to be great at something, but isn't?

Bottom line: Almost everybody on earth, at one time or another, has experienced the sick feeling of betrayal, and most of the time it leaves them dazed, despairing, and suspicious. They're not stronger or wiser, but simply reluctant to trust anybody—which can be crippling in and of itself.

To function effectively, humans must be able to predict what others will do, and trust them accordingly. But if you hand out your trust like candy, you can lose the things you treasure most. If there's any hint of that happening, you'll be tempted to close the doors you need to open, and you'll end up cold and alone in your own foreboding.

Fear, fear, fear. We've all been there.

Almost every primary fear in relationships, though, can be conquered by one of the mightiest of all human abilities: the power of accurate prediction. Without that power, you'll probably always be reluctant to trust—and you'll pay a steep price for that deficit. Trust creates a state of calm and creativity, animates everyone involved, and unites entire nations. It sits at the top of the human hierarchy of positive actions, because it is the action-equivalent of love—and often exists in combination with love.

When you're sizing people up, you learn a lot about their character, traits, tendencies, desires, fears, affections, strengths, weaknesses, and skills, but all of that feeds into the single most important attribute that you're invariably looking for: trustworthiness. It's the one quality that strips away mystery, illuminates the truth, and is indispensable to a positive relationship.

The Six Signs for Behavior Prediction

In this book, I'm going to show you my six-sign system for verifying trust—and the tells that reveal those signs—by predicting human behavior.

Here's a bird's-eye view of what you're going to learn:

Sign #1: Vesting
Creating symbiotic linkage of mutual success.

Sign #2: Longevity
Believing your bond will last.

Sign #3: Reliability
Demonstrating competence and diligence.

Sign #4: Actions
Displaying consistent patterns of positive behaviors.

Sign #5: Language
Creating connections with masterful communication.

Sign #6: Stability
Transcending conflict with emotional accord.

This system replaces guesswork, gut feelings, luck, intuition, and drama.

Many of the greatest fears that make life so difficult can be tamed by this simple system, and it can reveal the right path in most relationships.

The system isn't a popularity contest, nor even a measure of good or bad, but only *predictability*. It consists of reading the tells that accurately reflect somebody's character, traits, and abilities.

If you can trust somebody to do something you need, that's fine, and you can adjust your actions accordingly. But even if you find that you cannot trust someone to do something you need, that's also fine, because you can, again, *adjust your actions accordingly.*

The system won't solve all your problems, but because it confers the power of prediction, it will enable you to approach your decisions about whom to trust rationally and wisely, free from fear. It will help protect you from scam artists—including those in the C-suites—and will limit the time you lose to manipulators, flakes, phonies, and the well-meaning people who want to do what you trust them to, but just aren't able to.

Even better, the system will lead you to the *right* people: those who truly want you to succeed, have the ability to help, and will do whatever they can to make it happen. With them at your side, your worries will subside, your workload will lighten, your relationships will deepen, and your ability to predict your own future—and thus *create* it—will become phenomenal.

My system works because it cuts to the core of human behavior and rests primarily upon a single fundamental truth: *The one thing that you can almost always predict people to do is to act in their own best interests.*

Some people think that's cynical, but I think it's not only healthy, but necessary. It's the heart and soul of human survival, the wellspring of achievement, the hallmark of authenticity, and it can include any number of virtuous, altruistic goals.

The simple principle that *people try to get what they want* is so sensible, and so embedded into our culture and our psyches, that we tend to believe that people who don't act in their own best interests are self-destructive, lazy, or indifferent to the needs of those who depend upon them.

So to determine how people will act, you simply need to learn what they think is in their own best interests, and use that knowledge to predict their behavior. That's not always easy, but you can learn how. Quickly. And your life will never be the same. The power of prediction is a virtual superpower.

Trust, therefore, is not a matter of morality. Trust is a predictability.

This widens the definition of trust, from assuming that people are usually good to assuming that people are generally so consistent about trying to get what they *want* that you can predict how they'll act.

But trust must rest upon rational reasons—and simply liking someone is not one of them. A sad fact of life is that most people lose more to those they love than to everybody else put together. And it's not because the person they love is evil. It's because they didn't trust wisely.

That's why data-based predictability is so important. Predictability comes first. Trust follows. If you can't reasonably predict what someone will do, you usually can't trust them.

With trust come its trademark behaviors: loyalty, helpfulness, kindness, honesty, reliability, and wisdom. They're almost always part of the package of the people you trust. So as a rule, if you can predict the quality of *trustworthiness* in a person, you will naturally and inevitably wish to ally yourself with them. And they will feel the same.

This core truth about predicting what people will do is the only thing that any of us can ever know with certainty about trust, and it's all we need to know.

But it's important not to use this truth for mere manipulation. If you do, you may still be able to find people who you can trust, *but they'll never trust you.* The world is already full of manipulators, and you do not want that label to apply to you.

The first step in putting this principle of prediction into action is to find out what people think is in their own best interests. Most people will be happy to tell you. Why wouldn't they? It's usually the best way for them to get what they want. So what somebody tells you, obviously, is usually the best tell there is.

But some people will be afraid that they'll look pushy, needy, offensive, or narcissistic. Even when that happens, though, you can still find out what they want. Agents in the section of the FBI that I was recently in charge of—the Behavioral Analysis Program (BAP)—do that every day, and I'll teach you how to think like a BAP agent: objectively, rationally, systematically, and free from emotional distractions. With that mindset, you can accurately analyze the most predictive data points of people's behavior: their actions, statements, body language, opinions, personal reputation, professional track record, and abilities.

Those tells are easier to spot than you might think, because people usually reveal their inner traits and ideas through relatively obvious actions, similar to the tells in a poker game. Good poker players don't just play the cards; they also play the people.

Predicting behavior isn't rocket science—but it is a social science, and requires you to apply the right equation of logic, strategy, skepticism, observational skills, and the ability to accept unwelcome truths.

It also requires empathy, because to truly understand people, you've got to temporarily drop your own perspective and look at the world—and yourself—through their eyes. If you do, you may not like how they see you—especially if it's negative, and not accurate—but you'll still be one step closer to the reality of the rest of the world, and that alone is enlightening and empowering.

Doing this difficult reality check requires the raw courage of stoicism and the kindness of empathy: two of the most powerful forces in human behavior. When these two qualities work in unison, they create a trait that I now describe as "stempathy." The quality of stempathy, I believe, is one of the most profoundly positive traits in human behavior, my primary area of expertise.

For centuries, the study of human behavior was mostly philosophical, but far more inarguable truths about it emerged when it became a social science.

The data-driven analysis of this relatively new science first emerged in the 1970s and has since been refined. Behavior is, in effect, a smoking gun that's in plain sight.

I first became fascinated by the science of behavior as an officer in the United States Marine Corps, an environment in which bad decisions about people can cost lives. As a commander in charge of more than two hundred marines and sixteen drill instructors at Parris Island, I tiptoed into the realm of predicting what people will do. But that was in a very controlled environment.

When I joined the FBI in 1997, I took every advanced course I could in social psychology and the science of relationship development, and had my first contact with the BAP. It was run by leaders who held the almost futuristic belief, back then, that criminal and espionage activities—and, by extension, business and personal problems—could be controlled far more effectively by diving into the white-hot core of human behavior than by applying only the blunt-force instruments of power, money, punishment, or withdrawal.

At that time, the BAP was largely unknown to most Americans, although it was later featured in several episodes of the TV show *Criminal Minds*. The BAP is part of the Behavioral Analysis Unit (BAU), a department that focuses on violent crime rather than counterespionage. The BAU has been portrayed in the book and film *The Silence of the Lambs,* as well as in TV shows like *Law & Order, Mindhunter,* and *The Wire.* One reason it's a popular subject is because people intuitively know that they *shouldn't rely on intuition.* Life's too short, and we've all got too much to lose.

From early on, my professional dream was to be part of the BAP, because I believed it would not only empower my service to the country, but also help me to become a better, more prosperous person, with fewer conflicts, less fear, and deeper relationships.

Initially, though, I depended upon it mostly as a survival system. Every business and industry has its own share of sharks, but the sharks in espionage and counterespionage are backed by the full force, finances, and munitions of the most powerful nations on earth. Although I was lucky enough to eventually become the third of the four people who have run the BAP, I struggled at first.

I wish I knew then what I know now.

September 12, 2001
New York City

Before dawn, we started pulling months of twelve-hour, seven-day shifts, starting with a search in the rubble for leads. We simultaneously worked "fingers-and-toes" duty in the World Trade Center rubble that had been hauled to the landfill on Staten Island, where we collected pieces of people while they were still identifiable as human.

As we arrived and went home in the dark each day—developing our own domestic sense of combat fatigue—the West Side Highway in Manhattan was lined with people and volunteers, solemnly applauding with gloved, muffled hands, and holding candles in the rain and snow from September to January. They handed us juice boxes, homemade sandwiches, respirators—anything that would make our day better. They also gave us notes and photos scrawled with messages like "Please find my daddy." I still have every bit of it. It reminds me not only of those people, but of the deprivation my own kids felt as I was called away during that turbulent time.

None of us considered refusing the food, even after someone began to send notable people packages that contained the potent poison anthrax. We thought people deserved our trust and that their virtuous behavior was so predictable that we could bet our lives on it. I doubt I would do that now—or even get the chance to, because these days cops would probably cordon off the crowds.

Four years later, the FBI traced the anthrax to a suspect who'd worked for the federal government. We closed the case shortly after America invaded Iraq—in a war about weapons of mass destruction that didn't, in fact, exist—and the revelation that the anthrax had come from a government worker wasn't greeted with any great sense of irony by the public. America had changed.

By midwinter, most Americans were weary with their own version of combat fatigue—compassion fatigue—and a new level of wariness set in, limiting air travel to such a degree that two major carriers went bankrupt. People shifted so far away from seeing new places and seeking new friends that the word "cocooning" was coined.

A blanket of distrust had descended and still, for the most part, remains.

December 23, 2001
Long Island, New York

On this gray day in the winter of our discontent, I was tasked with following leads that would rule out Russian complicity. It made sense on one level, because everybody in the office was working 9/11 leads, and I'd been working Russia since I'd started.

A supervisor put me in touch with a secret informant who worked Russian counterintelligence for us—a Confidential Human Source (CHS), in spy-talk—and this person had flatly refused to talk about 9/11 with his current handler. That was his fourteenth agent, and I was going to be the fifteenth. The CHS—whom we'll call Leo, for our purposes here—had been a double agent for years, but he had a reputation for walking a fine line between helping us and helping himself. Somebody even said he might be connected with the new Russian entrepreneurial class later called the Russian Mafia. We did know that he owned some kind of gentleman's club for Russian expatriates. That alone was enough to generate rumors, and in this chaotic moment in history no rumor was too wild. Even if he was legit, I hated his way of operating. It seemed selfish and narrow, like the mindset of a mercenary whose only loyalty is to the highest bidder. But that's not how I would feel these days, because I've realized that a lasting, valid transaction with anybody—including a CHS—has to be win-win.

It took me two hours to drive out to Leo's comfortable Dutch colonial near the woodsy part of West Babylon on Long Island, and by the time I got there, about fifteen hours into my workday, my nerves were shot. As I stood on Leo's porch, he fumbled open the door, acting and smelling like he was drunk.

So here I was, trying to *save the whole damn world,* and he was wasting my time. Pissed me off. It didn't take much that winter.

Instead of stepping aside for me to enter, he said, "This is the last time I will see you here," as he glanced up and down the block.

"Why?" Was he pissed off himself? *Because* he sensed my anger? Probably. He had penetrating eyes, drunk or not.

"Neighbors," he said.

"I think maybe you're being a little *paranoid,* sir." That was putting it mildly, I thought, but it felt good to give him some shit. This was back in the days when I thought that venting was emotionally healthy. These days, I'd never say something like that—not because I'm Miss Manners, but because it serves no purpose. And good managers—in any business—don't piss away words on casual observations. Every letter of every word they say moves them closer to their ultimate goal.

Leo reared back a little and said, in his part-Russian, part-Queens accent, "Ya got a big mouth on ya."

That's why I'd never say it now. When you talk shit, you get shit. More on that later. Besides, "just being yourself" is overrated. If you can't bring your best self to a meeting, stay away.

I stood my ground, as would any good marine or FBI agent—or so I thought. I just wanted to get the hell in, get the hell out, and cross Leo off my list.

He opened the door wider and motioned me to his family room, which had an elaborate bar. Leo plopped four ice cubes into his drink, and said, "I was in a prison camp after World War II, and learned to love ice. We had none. Of course." He topped it off with more vodka. "Drink?"

I shook my head.

"Although," he continued, "they called the camp a Displaced Persons Center. Although nobody was being 'placed.' All told, there were about ten million of us living behind barbed wire. For five years I was there. Almost always hungry. And when I would ask about going back to my village, to see if my family was still alive, they would tell me to not be . . . what was your word? So *paranoid*. They would say, 'Don't worry about something you cannot control.' It made no sense. We have no need to worry about what we can control. The danger comes from the things we can't."

"Did you get back to your village?"

"Eventually. But on my own penny." His eyes grew vacant for a moment. "Only the ground was there. With rubble." He didn't elaborate on the survival of his family, and I didn't pry. If I knew then what I know now, I *would* pry—but delicately, and strictly for the benefit of the other person. When you give more to people, you get more. Back then, I would have thought that was ironic.

The Russians, he clearly wanted me to know, as he swirled his drink, had suffered twenty million deaths in World War II, compared to America's half million. *Forty times* the suffering, if you can imagine. "That is why we took over Eastern Europe," he said. "We were *paranoid*. But even with the buffer of the Iron Curtain, twenty million more people were killed by Jughashvili. That was Stalin's real name, until he became a politician. Stalin means 'Son of Steel.' So Comrade Jughashvili also made us"—he paused for effect and drew out the word—"paranoid."

So the war, plus Stalin, brought the sum of Russia's suffering to *eighty* times that of America. I must have looked sheepish, because for the first time he smiled, but it was the creepy kind.

I wanted to get down to business. "I understand that you're not happy with your current contact at the Bureau," I said.

"It's always *busy-ness* first with the FBI," he said, his face looking dead.

Another insult—which in my dumb-ass, near-rookie mind meant: *Fire back!*

"What I've heard about you," I said—in full combat mode, with little to lose—"is that to *give* something, you've got to *get* something. It's almost like—" I had to pause, because this was a nasty shot. "Like you're a double agent."

"All agents, my young friend, are double agents."

And that was the end of that.

But only from my point of view—which, I was soon to discover, was absolutely irrelevant, because the only thing that mattered right then was *his* point of view. Staying stuck in your own perceptions, I've found, is like having a long conversation with no one there. Save your breath.

By picking a fight with him, I was in over my head—which I thought at the time was the best way to learn how to swim with the sharks. That's how far in over my head I was.

I had almost learned to think like an agent over the past few years, but I hadn't learned how to think like a Behavioral Analysis agent.

Dark hit early and hard. It always does at that time of year, although people usually feel sheltered from the specter of darkness by the approach of the holidays. But this was a bad winter, and the spring held no promise.

I was getting nowhere. From Leo's file alone, I had innumerable data points, but none of them revealed who he really was or what he'd do next. Confusion reigned.

I wasn't alone. Much of the Bureau, and even the country, had been blinded by the same shared fog of cold war. Our enemies seemed to be everywhere, but we didn't even know who they were.

Even the three-letter agencies had limited knowledge of who would strike next, how they would come at us, or whom we could trust.

In this seemingly endless holding pattern, the best-case scenario for me and a lot of other New Yorkers seemed to be the luxury of simply surviving until we died of old age. People were sick all over town—especially in lower Manhattan—and were still breathing air so filthy that it would soon cause even more deaths than the collapse of the World Trade Center itself. Fires were still burning underground, fed by approximately 24,000 gallons of jet fuel, 100,000 tons of rotting debris, and 230,000 gallons of heating and diesel oil.

I was still coughing up all kinds of crap, and the cough has never completely let go. Cancer was on people's minds. Realistically. About ten thousand first responders now have various cancers and deadly diseases, and the toll will climb throughout our lifetimes.

Leo freshened his drink and again offered me one, which may or may not have meant he was trying to bridge our gap.

"I have something to tell you," he said, too loudly, as drunk people sometimes do.

Then I heard a man call out something that sounded a lot like, "Dead!" Was it "Dad," but with a Russian accent? Doubtful. Leo's folder said that his only son had died in the Soviet Union's war with Afghanistan.

Even so, after working fingers-and-toes, and looking everywhere for new threats, even seasoned agents were jumping to unlikely conclusions, based only on paranoia.

Agents aren't supposed to think like that. They're supposed to remain rational and believe only objective, observable *facts*. But a *lot* of things were happening that weren't supposed to.

Leo looked alarmed. "You must go now," he said, nodding toward his front door and hurrying down a hallway.

I looked behind me as I walked to my car in the dark. *Paranoid?* At this point in my life—which was headed inevitably toward death, and sure to include more suffering, as every life does—I agreed with Leo on the concept of paranoia: Who invented *that* happy bullshit? Whoever did must have been lucky as hell to feel so fearless. Or was crazy.

DEBRIEFING

CHAPTER 1:
"PREVAIL IN A WORLD OF STRANGERS"

Key Quote: "Few of the most serious problems in life are as common as not being able to read people, and accurately predict what they'll do."

Key Message: Sizing people up—to predict what they'll probably do—has become so obscured by myths, misinformation, and matters of morality that many people make bad choices. Some simple behavioral analysis rules make it far more accurate and easy.

THE TAKEAWAYS

A Framework for Predicting Behavior
- **Trust comes first:** The single most common—and important—reason for sizing someone up is to measure their trustworthiness: as an employee, a boss, a business associate, a teacher, a student, a friend, or a spouse. Trust lies at the heart of all human transactions.
- **Assume primacy of self-interests:** The one thing that you can almost always predict people to do is to act in their own best interests. It's healthy and rational, and is the wellspring of teamwork, achievement, and authenticity. It can, and often does, include a vast variety of virtuous, altruistic goals.
- **Trust is predictability, not morality:** This widens the definition of trust: from assuming that people are good to

assuming that people are so consistent about trying to get what they want that you can predict how they'll act.

- **Keep feelings out of it:** You can like someone and not trust them, and you can trust someone and not like them. A behavioral assessment based mostly on emotion will probably be incorrect. Predicting what people will do requires a rational, objective, nonjudgmental assessment of their behavior.

- **Look for signs of desperation:** When people are absolutely desperate, you can reasonably predict that they will do almost anything, including betraying you. But the opposite can also be predicted: When people are desperate, they will want to satisfy you and anyone else who might help them. Look for both in your data.

- *Doveryai no Proveryai:* **Trust, but verify:** Sometimes people mislead you on purpose, and sometimes by accident. Even when you trust somebody, make a reasonable effort to check on what they say.

2

THINK LIKE AN FBI BEHAVIORAL ANALYST

December 24, 2001
Beyond Betrayal

It was the night before Christmas, and everybody in the office was on edge. It would be the perfect time for terrorists to hit again, with millions of people shopping or celebrating, the churches jam-packed, and the public freaking out about the underground fires still spewing soot and fumes at Ground Zero. The attack wouldn't be done for any tactical military advantage, but just for the drama. Terrorists, along with the millions of people who manipulate with fear, love drama. I hate it.

Because our building was temporarily inoperable, we were based just off the West Side Highway on the World War II aircraft carrier *Intrepid*. Everybody was working 9/11 leads as our families waited at home, without complaint. Most of our children were aware of such sad things as the Christmas party in a firehouse near us, organized to give some comfort to the kids of the fifteen firefighters of that house who'd died on 9/11.

Fear was fogging the views of most Americans—New Yorkers especially—even though many of their fears, such as those in rural areas, seemed to be irrational.

Only the most rational people, as usual, were spared from unnecessary fear. But on the morning after my unusual meeting with Leo, I wasn't in that lucky group.

Even so, the first thing I did on the day after meeting Leo was to find out if he had someone else living in his home, which could account for somebody calling out something that sounded like "Dead!"

He did have a housemate: a twenty-year-old grandson who worked in the city, similarly to Leo. I also found out that the Russian word for grandfather was *ded*, with a slight *y* sound in it: *dyet*. It helped to know that. But only a little.

My problem was that even after several years in the Bureau, I was still thinking like a marine too often. Soldiers are trained to expect the unexpected, since they work in situations designed for that. But agents don't assume anything until they collect objective, observable, rational data, free from emotions—including the most destructive emotion: fear. This often takes us to the most predictable scenario. If you're a businessperson, this method will almost certainly be effective, since business is fundamentally based on the profit motive, which makes predictions much simpler.

Physicians use a very similar system as they complete a workup of their patient, often arriving at the most predictable diagnosis. Their phrase for describing the relative genius of seeing the obvious is, "Think horses, not zebras"—in other words, focus on the most obvious conclusion.

Regardless of the profession, applying a rational, systematic approach is much wiser than being influenced by fears, illusions, and unlikely catastrophes. I call that kind of hyperemotional, pointless pursuit "emotional hijacking."

Leo seemed to be pushing me down the path of emotional hijacking—possibly into a trap—which may have been sprung on the fourteen guys before me. It seemed as if my options had suddenly dwindled to keeping my distance—and getting blamed for lack of effort—or sucking up to him and waiting for him to make me look like a fool or a failure, for God knows what reason.

My job, of course, was to find out that reason. But I wasn't God.

Trying to size Leo up made me feel young again, but not in a good way. As a kid, I often felt victimized by betrayal, and did what most people do: blame the people who betrayed me, try to crawl away from the damage, and vow to never let it happen again.

But it did, and every time felt like the first: stunning, insulting, and bewildering. Informed only by the slender wisdom of youth, I thought that if I toughened up and strictly limited my affection and affiliation, I'd never again be caught by surprise.

Like so many people, I ended friendships, quit jobs, broke off romantic relationships, held grudges, nursed anger, and fantasized about retribution. Needless to say, when adolescence hit, all of that turned into a full-time job.

As I matured, I overcame those reflexive responses, but only because they didn't help, but just created further isolation and alienation.

Even then, though, I had neither a strategy nor a philosophy to fill the void. Everywhere I looked, I still saw people who were needy, scheming, and indifferent to what anyone else wanted. It didn't occur to me that I was basically the same way, and called it ambition.

Because I'm an optimist by nature, each new day dawned with the dream that life would be different and that I would soon meet the storied people who kept all their promises, always came through in a crisis, told me nothing but the truth, and worked as hard for me as I did for them.

But that didn't change the way that life worked. Life has, so to speak, an agenda of its own, and sometimes life's very marrow presents challenges, no matter what you do. The cause of these challenges shifts its shape from era to era and person to person, but rarely strays far from the primal, simple necessity of survival, with a dream of prosperity.

But even the simplicity that once governed survival and prosperity in America is gone now, because the demands of the global economy present historic uncertainty. Battling in this new ultracompetitive arena is a fight against people we rarely meet, in places we've never been. And the pleasures of control and predictability are as distant and amorphous as rainbows.

For the remainder of your life, only the details of this will change. It's simply reality, and like the entirety of reality, it's neither good nor bad: It just is.

The wealthiest one percent of us can hide from this reality, but the rest of us, who live in what we like to call the real world, must forge our alliances wherever we can, and adapt, to the best of our abilities, to the real-world truths about the human race. Some of these truths are hard to accept.

THE HARD TRUTHS ABOUT PREDICTING BEHAVIOR

Variability: Almost everyone's behavior is highly variable, depending upon a person's degree of desperation, their degree of temptation, and the degree of punishment that they will face if they violate trust or other rules of conduct.

Immunity: When people have immunity from consequences—due to wealth, power, or status—it tends to have a strong negative effect on their behavior.

Vulnerability: The people who are the easiest to predict tend to be those who are the most vulnerable, because they are the easiest to punish for violating rules of proper conduct.

Incompetence: One of the most common reasons people fail to behave in a predictable way is not because they don't want to, but because they're unable to, no matter how hard they try.

The 50 Percent Rule: The conventional rate of accurately predicting trustworthiness, and its altruistic components, has never been higher than approximately 50 percent.

Intuition: This is the most common method for predicting trust and the virtues that go with it. It's also the least reliable. Intuition can enable people to have more empathy, but it's generally not an effective tool for discerning how well people will behave, because it's too easy to confuse simply liking people with being able to predict their behavior—especially when they're the most desperate or tempted.

Appearances: Many of the most common social and professional factors that are used to determine virtuous, helpful behavior are virtually irrelevant. These include someone's religious and political affiliations, their projection of confidence, their physical proximity, their appearance, and their elevated professional status. These factors, often subjective, can be inviting and pleasing. They're great for the comfort factor. But they lack the efficacy of objective, data-driven assessments.

Longevity: When people believe that they will have only a short relationship with you, it's harder to predict what they'll do. Duration creates a much more compelling climate for reward—or punishment.

Perceptions: Your own perception of someone's situation does not make it easier to predict what they'll do. To accurately size them up, you've got to go with *their* perceptions. (Unless they're a veritable Mini-Me—which some people pretend to be, in order to manipulate you.)

Persistence: When you're sizing someone up, you can be relentless in the pursuit of truth without triggering retribution or resistance, as long as you make it clear that *you understand why* they are the way they are. If they think you're judging them, they'll clam up. If you persist, you're much more likely to see the worst side of them.

Trust: There's a reason I keep coming back to trust. Trustworthiness is the fulcrum upon which all accurate, actionable knowledge of a person rests—and without it, you'll never quite know where you stand with them.

An important caveat: Each of these basic rules—no matter how generally true—has many exceptions, and to presume they apply in all cases would be not only unfair, but unproductive. The most important thing to remember is that many people rise to positions of power and influence *because they are virtuous and trustworthy.*

December 27, 2001
Sizing Up Leo

I came to the wide-open office door of Jesse Thorne, a veteran agent I'd come to see as my mentor—or, more accurately, my Jedi Master, because his lessons often seemed effortless and allegorical—and said, "Knock knock."

"Hey, Robin, come on in." He didn't look busy. He never did.

"Do you ever close your door?" I asked.

"Don't need to. I had my office designated as a Drama Free Zone."

"Must be nice."

"It's boring. That's my favorite emotion. It makes things happen. Contrary to popular opinion."

Jesse had received the Bureau's greatest honor, the Director's Award—twice. He typically worked the most cataclysmic cases, but you'd never know it, because of his laid-back style and the complete lack of framed certificates on the wall behind his desk—the traditional Wall of Ego that most of the older guys had. His only office adornment was an orange juice can that held his cheap ballpoint pens. His award certificates, he'd once told me, were in a shoe box in his basement that his kids used as a puck for broom hockey.

I'd learned more from Jesse than from all the specialized courses on behavioral analysis and spycraft combined, including counterintelligence interviewing, espionage investigations, false flags, crisis negotiation, statement analysis, undercover operations, and spy recruitment.

"Jesse, what do you know about the CHS they call Leo?"

"Probably nothing you don't. I heard he got assigned to you."

"Yeah, but why? How could a guy like him have anything to do with the WTC cases we've got open?"

"You should ask him." Jesse always had easy answers to hard questions. At the time, that seemed odd to me—even unprofessional.

"I can't break down his barriers," I said. "Brick wall."

"I heard he does that. He's just testing you. To see if you're just another ambitious asshole."

I was dubious. "So those fourteen other guys were assholes?"

"What I mean is, that's how *he* feels. That's all that matters."

"But it's not true."

"So . . . ?" He gave me his quizzical look that said, *I'm bewildered by your stupidity but much too kind to mention it.* He always got away with that, because he packaged his criticism in a way that implied he and everybody, including him, was in the same boat. We were all brothers and sisters in the mysteries of humankind.

"So what do I do?"

"Find out where that nickname Leo came from!" He shrugged. "I'm just curious."

I waited. He scooted back from his desk and continued, as if he'd given it a great deal of thought: "Stay rational and nonjudgmental about his opinions of you or anybody else. Break the ice. And be nice—that's the main thing. Always."

"I've gotten better advice from a fortune cookie."

He laughed—at himself. "I'm just saying, don't f**k yourself up," he said. "You're too good at it. We're *all* too good at it, because we all know exactly which of our own *buttons* to push—and that 'skill' makes us our *own best enemies.* A little of it is okay, because it keeps us on our toes. But when you get too hung up on your own faults, people can tell, and it makes you hard to trust. So go ahead and let Leo be the bad guy. Because if you let him, he probably won't do it. Nice guys never finish last. In fact, they don't finish," he said, drilling a deep look into me.

(You're probably getting a sense of where the Jedi thing came from.)

"This is key, too," he said. "Ask not what Leo can do for you. Ask what you can do for Leo."

"But that's why the other guys didn't like him. He's always playing both sides!"

"They probably didn't offer him anything. That's why he *asked:* to show them what not to do. It's just simple negative psychology."

The double negatives were starting to stack up.

"Get in his head," Jesse said. "By being a resource for what he wants. When you're playing his role and he's playing yours, that's a tell of predictable, trustworthy behavior."

I actually understood that. Which worried me a little. But Jesse could see that I got it, and beamed.

"Remind me," he said. "Did I mention, don't talk shit?"

"Not this time." I'd heard it before. It meant: limit myself to nonjudgmental, validating statements, be an active listener, and above all stay logical, even in the face of sarcasm, insults, or anger. Easier said than done, right? He paused, but I was lost again.

Assume you can trust him. "Make him know that you're in the *Leo* business! And that he's stuck with you—for the long haul."

That made sense. But it was so obvious.

"Did I say, be nice?" he asked.

"Yeah." Was he testing me? Or was I really that dumb? Or both?

"Good! If you do all that, he'll probably mirror you—match you—and then you'll be able to tell when he's on the level and that he can do what he says he can. And that he can't do what he says he can't. Sooo . . . yeah! There you go!"

I felt like I'd just listened to the worst TED Talk in history. But I didn't say so. I was nice.

That was my first smart move on the case. What Jesse had just told me was the seed for my eventual system for sizing people up. I think I'd heard most of it before, but now it was starting to sink in.

So let's delve further into those six signs I told you about in the beginning.

THE SIX SIGNS FOR BEHAVIOR PREDICTION

Sign #1. Vesting: Does this person believe they will benefit from your success?

If they do, it's one of the most positive signs in all of human behavior. More than any other quality—including, sometimes, even love—it signifies partnership and commitment.

This belief is relatively common among couples and families, but it's also present in many business partnerships and some temporary working relationships.

When the people whose behavior you're sizing up see your achievements as a positive reflection on themselves, they'll take great pains to help you however they can. So this sign creates *pure power of prediction.*

They'll voluntarily link themselves to you, protect you from harm, and find ways to promote your interests.

I like to vest in the success of as many people as is reasonably possible, because when I do, they usually vest in *my* success—as well as the success of others close to me—and my effectiveness increases exponentially.

Like most of the six signs, this perception must be how the *other* person feels, and not just how you feel. If they don't see it, it doesn't exist—even if it should. Some people shy away from promising alliances, because they still believe in the proverbial Army of One. But the Army of One almost always gets its ass kicked by the Army of Two. An Army of Three tops an Army of Two. Do the math.

To find out if somebody would be a good ally, talk to them about their immediate goals, necessities, concerns, and passions, and see if they fit with yours. If they do, tell them. They'll probably jump all over it. The urge for partnership is a primal need.

But if you do need to persuade somebody to be your ally, don't bother. They need to see for themselves that they'll benefit—and *want* to. Then they'll go all in. I'd rather work with a few people giving me 100 percent than a hundred people giving me 50 percent.

Sign #2. Longevity: Does this person think they will have a long relationship with you?

Time equals trust.

If people think they will be linked with you for a long time, they'll be very motivated to build a mutually beneficial relationship with you, and you'll be able to predict their important moves. They'll make sacrifices for you, because they know there's time for you to return the favor.

Short relationships invite exploitation. When someone thinks their relationship with you will soon be over, they won't see much opportunity in it. They'll face only a short period of enduring the consequences or sharing the gains. So most of the time, you won't know what's next with them.

If people think they'll be dealing with you for a long time, though—whether by choice, happenstance, or assignment—they will be far more likely to care about your opinion of them and more apt to believe that you can help them. They'll try harder to fulfill their promises and act in your best interests.

It's very common for strangers to become friends and allies when they know that their fates are linked, or even when they know that they will be associating with one another for at least a year or two.

It's also often wise to extend a relationship even after the ostensible objective is achieved. All you've got to say is, "You seem like somebody I'd like to get to know better, so keep in touch!"

Then follow through. The future lasts a long time.

Sign #3. Reliability: Can this person do what they say they will? And *will* they?

You can't predict how someone will act if they don't show signs of *reliability,* a quality that's composed of *competence* and *diligence.*

Just because someone wants to do something for you, it doesn't mean they're competent to do it. And even if they are, it doesn't mean they're diligent enough to get the job *done.*

False claims of competence are most commonly due to lack of self-awareness, which can surface as arrogance, deceit, and sometimes optimism. It's common for type-A people to think they can do things better than they really can, so it's important to get data points on specific skills and achievements.

It's also common for people to exaggerate their abilities and achievements, either to keep up with others or because they think *others will be exaggerating, too.*

Some people simply aren't realistic with themselves about their capabilities. Many well-meaning people of good character overrate themselves, an action that's pandemic in many professions.

Sometimes it's just because they'd be reluctant to attempt something if they were more realistic with themselves. Underestimation of difficulty is, ironically, a survival skill.

So optimism—as opposed to realism—is usually not closely tied to predictability.

Similarly, it's easy for the person assessing positive behaviors to be overly optimistic, and believe that others will be more competent than they are, due to wishful thinking.

Other factors can also affect reliability, such as family obligations, health issues, and work.

Reliability also depends on someone's degree of diligence: their willpower, work ethic, sense of responsibility, willingness to graciously accept unwelcome assignments, and ability to make changes. It's important to assess the *full scope* of a person's life, career, and worldview before you become their ally.

Reliability is a dealbreaker. Don't hesitate to insist on evidence. *Doveryai no Proveryai:* Trust, but verify.

Sign #4. Actions: Does this person consistently demonstrate patterns of positive behavior?

This action-based sign is very important, because what people *do* is almost always more revealing than what they *say.*

Actions are especially indicative of predictable, trustworthy behavior when they back up prior claims, because this shows that people are serious about doing what they say they'll do.

When their actions don't match what they say, stay away.

But somebody's *past* patterns of behavior are not a foolproof indicator of how they'll be in the future. That's especially true when all you know about them is what they tell you.

Résumés, for example, can be very misleading, because they're created by the least objective person involved. And sometimes former employers and other references are overly kind in their evaluations, since they won't suffer the consequences of the sugarcoating themselves. Also, résumés rarely reveal what people will do when new forms of duress or temptation arise.

However, the internet has made it harder for people to fudge their résumés, and social media holds a trove of information about most people.

Past patterns of various character issues—such as honesty, effectiveness, and fairness—are especially poor at predicting current trustworthy behavior.

People who are explicitly informed that they will be held responsible for their actions are much more likely to adhere to their own past patterns of positive behavior.

Even so, current behavior—including very recent behavior in a similar situation—is almost always more important than what happened in the past.

Among the most important current behaviors that indicate positive character traits are: honest communication, lack of secrecy, consistency between actions and the descriptions of the actions; transparency about actions; signs of diligence; and descriptions of past or current actions that are simple and unadorned. Plain talk is good, because simplicity reveals and complexity conceals.

Sign #5. Language: Does this person know how to communicate in a positive way? Or do they talk trash?

A surprisingly large number of people think they can enforce their agendas, and even ingratiate themselves, by talking trash: blaming others, being rude or bombastic, exaggerating, manipulating, using debating tactics, or being hyperemotional and evasive. Even when people are careful not to aim these verbal weapons directly at you, it's still a strong indication of negative behavior. A person's negative communication style primarily reflects their fear, but it usually comes out sounding angry and hurtful—even if it's couched in humor. Some managers seem to think it's appropriate to talk smack as an expression of their own toughness, down-to-earthness, candor, or honesty.

Even so, everything you need to communicate could also be said with tact, understanding, and rationalism. You can be absolutely straightforward if you address people with respect and a desire to understand them.

Language often unveils the realities that lie behind people's words, especially when it is deep and simple rather than shallow and complex.

The single most revealing linguistic method for measuring character is to monitor people's language for nonjudgmental, validating statements about others.

People who talk far more about themselves than others are also hard to size up, since the essence of healthy alliances is sharing.

A person's language style not only reflects their degree of positive traits, but can also *create* it, in accord with René Descartes's philosophy that "we do not describe the world we see; we see the world we describe." Helpful, positive behavior is contagious, and the best way to spread it is with the words you say.

Unreliable and unpredictable people often try to say the right things with the right words, but are usually exposed by subtle signs of the disconnect between their words and their actions.

This can be revealed by the rapid rate of speech among "fast talkers" or by the manipulative speech of "smooth talkers." People also often reveal themselves with slightly understated bragging, ambiguity, passive-aggressiveness, or begging for compliments.

You can usually predict kind, friendly behavior among people who are better listeners than speakers. After all, we have two ears and one mouth, so we should listen twice as much as we speak.

Effective communicators ask a lot of questions, are easy to understand, don't try to manipulate, and are almost always looking for ways to connect.

Finding good people through speech is fairly simple: When you hear it, you'll know it.

Sign #6. Stability: Does this person consistently demonstrate emotional maturity, self-awareness, and social skills?

Many good people just don't have the emotional stability to do the things that others need from them, and it makes them unreliable and unpredictable. A person's instability may stem from prior trauma, biochemical imbalances, excessive stress, substance abuse, emotional or physical abuse, or exhaustion—often occurring in combination.

Occasionally, though, people are just emotionally lazy and indulge gratuitously in behaviors that other people rise above, such as complaining, whining, finding fault, criticizing, pouting, and punishing.

Compassion is important, but I believe that we have no moral obligation to encumber our own duties and dreams in order to serve the needs of people whose emotional instability limits their opportunity to be predictable and acceptable.

The most fatal flaw to predicting emotionally imbalanced people is that sometimes they think they're acting in their own best interests but are not. When people intermittently operate as their own best enemies, it's almost impossible to know what to expect from them.

This is a relatively common problem these days, because our current culture is characterized by reflexive, hyperemotional polarization, which promotes further cynicism and confrontation. In an environment in which vitriolic reactions are triggered by prosaic problems, emotional stability is a necessity for predictably positive behavior.

Nobody is perfect, though, and when you are assessing the predictability of someone who has moderate emotional flaws—as so many of us do—you can still accurately predict what they'll do by establishing a baseline of their behavior and then being alert for deviations from that norm. For example, if you propose an idea to someone who is typically pessimistic, it's not necessarily a problem if they're pessimistic about your idea. It's just how they are, and you can rely on them to stay that way—and you don't have to give up on your idea.

Fortunately, emotional stability exists on a continuum. Most people are adequately stable, while others have abundant emotional stability, characterized by empathy, rationality, emotional control, consistency, communication skills, and acumen for social interaction.

These people are usually easy to predict and partner with, if your interests align with theirs. But not always. So, final strategy: Deepen your *own* emotional stability—and you might be surprised at how stable others become.

Those are the bare-bones basics of the **Six Signs for Behavior Prediction**—absolutely none of which I knew back in the dark days after 9/11, when I thought I knew a great deal about trust, but knew very little. Luckily, I had some good teachers.

The End of History

I headed toward my second meeting with Leo, driving slowly through the benign gauntlet of grieving people, with my car window rolled down, smelling the residue of burned wreckage that seemed as if it would forever foul the air of New York.

Emily, a volunteer from New Jersey, reached out from the sidewalk and handed me a bottle of Gatorade along with a note that said, "Thank you for saving America." In my exhaustion and despair, Emily's kindness made me sick with guilt. Every day, my work felt like a matter of life and death, and every night I knew I hadn't achieved a *single damn thing* that could help *anybody*. I remember sitting in traffic, thinking: *My God! I'm totally useless!*

Jesse's pep talk had helped, but I hadn't yet had time to test out his ideas.

It was the low point in my career, and to a large extent at this time, my career was my life. After four years in the Bureau, preceded by five years in the Marine Corps and four years at the Naval Academy, I could no more save America than I could fly.

But the destruction of my dreams left me with nothing to lose, and my mindset shifted, as if on its own, and settled in a place that said it was acceptable to *help one person at a time.* It felt like neither capitulation nor epiphany. It just felt like a promise I'd made to myself deep in the past but had long forgotten in my dreams of grandeur.

I would start with Leo. If he was sober enough to accept it.

He was, but he looked like he had a hangover—and was anxious to start working on his next one. The winter sun was plummeting, soot lay on the snow like a black blanket, and the dark, sour-smelling bar where we met felt like one more embodiment of my failure and America's gloom. When I sat down, Leo's face was so dark and creased with the history of his pain that I forgot about my rehearsed questions and blurted, "Is there something I can do for you?"

He didn't say anything, and I didn't either, because I just didn't have the energy.

Finally, he said slowly, "Do you know anything about visa extensions?"

I nodded, and then I learned about the life of "The Lion," Leo's nickname in the Soviet secret police—due to his physical bulk and personal power. It was the only employment option he was offered, as a way to leave the postwar displacement gulag. He'd been forced to do things for the KGB that would fill any sane person with lifelong shame, and he vowed at the time to someday redeem his soul by risking everything for the cause of freedom, which he had so seldom experienced.

Trying to comprehend, I asked some dumb question about the mystery of survivor's guilt, and with a look of terrible amusement at my naivete, he said, "It's not because you survive, young man, but what you *do* to survive. A little manipulation for a better job here, a piece of stolen bread there, a secret hiding place that was not big enough to share. The strong do not survive, my young friend. Only the wily."

Leo had lost his only son in the Soviet war with Afghanistan, his first wife to breast cancer, and most of his money to bureaucrats who'd managed to survive the Soviet collapse by allying themselves with gangsters. His only family now was his second wife and his grandson, Viktor, a bicycle messenger who had been hit by a car in the melee on 9/11 and inhaled enough toxins while lying on a sidewalk for twelve hours to make his lungs fill with water and blood. I had a slight frame of reference for that, because my lungs were also damaged that day.

Leo's insurance company was inundated with 9/11 claims, and he'd spent the last dollar he had on out-of-pocket medical expenses—with no assurance of reimbursement—and his grandson's visa was expiring.

"Was it Viktor who I heard calling out to you?"

He nodded. "He's very afraid," Leo said, his voice cracking with sorrow. "If he's sent back to Russia, his medical care will probably end."

I bought Leo a drink. Then I said, "I have a few friends. Let me see what I can do." Somehow he knew that I really meant it.

"That would be greatly appreciated," he said.

My offer didn't feel like an obligation to me. It felt like freedom—in the most American of ways. It was a personal connection offered freely, which could not be dissolved by any decree of government, business, or religion.

Leo gulped his drink and told me that he would introduce me to "another member of the club"—meaning an asset in counterintelligence—who supposedly had information about secret al-Qaeda sanctuaries in a former Soviet state.

It felt like we were finally building a predictable, trust-based relationship. I didn't feel at all manipulated, and he didn't, either.

I lifted my drink and said, *"Doveryai no Proveryai."* He repeated it and clinked his glass with mine.

His al-Qaeda claim was astonishing to me, as my offer to help probably was to him. But we both knew that we'd be working together to help his grandson, so we shared that mission. We also knew it would take at least a year for his grandson to heal, so I would have plenty of time to see if Leo was reliable—and vice versa. I never doubted his competence, and his diligence would be supercharged by his concern for his grandson. I was certain he'd soon feel the same way about my reliability, after I solved his grandson's visa problem and helped him navigate some federal programs that provided 9/11 medical care.

As I saw a different side of him, I realized that beneath his wounded exterior he was a sensitive man with true wisdom, hiding a heart that had been badly hurt, but still had hope.

I knew from his past actions that he was nothing if not a survivor, and that his gift for survival—despite the guilt it caused him—could be transferred to others whose wounds were still raw and bloody.

In the fall and winter of 2001, which still seems near, a multitude of Americans tasted for the first time the bitter vulnerability that so much of the world suffers every day. Millions of us were still hiding our battered psyches in holes, trying to find a way to get past what had happened, and to crawl out—begin again—and learn to find the best in others, rather than fear the worst.

For these reasons and others, I trusted Leo to guide me on the most important work of my life.

Our friendship had begun.

The al-Qaeda operation was just the beginning—and would almost immediately lead to an event that threatened to do far more damage than the World Trade Center attacks.

When that happened, I was grateful to have such a dependable, predictable man by my side. I'm certain Leo felt the same. I didn't even have to ask.

A New Beginning

In the dark days after 9/11—gradually to grow brighter—the "*end* of history" was nevertheless *over*, and we were back into historic times, starting with what felt like a modern version of the Dark Ages.

Now 9/11 feels forever frozen in the American consciousness. It exists almost as a part of the present, in a surreal compartment in which time is measured not so much by when, but by who and what—and why.

It's said that if we don't remember history, we will be doomed to repeat it. So having a part of 9/11 frozen into so many people's memories should help keep us safe.

But humankind will *always* repeat history, no matter how well we remember it. We are, after all, only human. That is the lesson we learned during the short and precious moments when history seemed to cease.

So now we can say with sad certainty that history can never end, because people will keep making the same mistakes, again and again.

Can a prediction system such as mine remedy that? No. Not globally, nor eternally. Not a chance.

But it will help some people from making the same mistakes they've made before.

That's a start—and maybe all there is—but it's enough, at least for now.

For you, there is—with luck and work—a chance that your best days yet will soon begin.

DEBRIEFING

CHAPTER 2:
"THINK LIKE AN FBI BEHAVIORAL ANALYST"

Key Quote: "Agents don't assume anything until they collect objective, observable, rational data, free from emotions—including the most destructive emotion: fear."

Key Message: Sizing people up—with the behavioral science protocols that *predict how they will act*—has become so denatured by myths and matters of morality that its practical purposes have been obscured. *But any person can learn the fundamental skills of sizing people up in a matter of days, leading to insights of great value, both professionally and personally.*

The Hard Truths About Predicting Behavior
- **Variability:** The behavior of almost all people changes significantly throughout life, depending upon their situations, and their degree of control over their own lives.
- **Immunity:** People with notable power—which decreases their accountability—are sometimes tempted to behave badly, and often succumb to the temptation.
- **Vulnerability:** The actions of vulnerable people are the easiest to predict, because they are the most accountable.
- **Incompetence:** People often mislead others by making the honest mistake of thinking they can do things they can't.

- **The 50 Percent Rule:** The most common forms of predicting behavior—lacking the data points of behavioral science—are wrong approximately half the time.
- **Intuition:** Intuition is notably ineffective for predicting what someone will do.
- **Appearances:** People who share many situational similarities with you are often no easier to predict than anyone else.
- **Longevity:** Long-term relationships, by choice or by circumstance, make both parties more accountable, and therefore predictable.
- **Perceptions:** Predicting what people will do depends primarily on *their* perceptions, not yours.
- **Persistence:** People who are the most manipulative often masquerade as the most virtuous and trustworthy.
- **Trust:** Trust—based on objective, observable actions such as honesty and transparency—is the most important value in most human transactions.

The Six Signs for Behavior Prediction

1. **Vesting:** People's belief that they will benefit from your success.
2. **Longevity:** People's belief that they will have a long relationship with you.
3. **Reliability:** People's observable, quantifiable degrees of competence and diligence.
4. **Actions:** People's present behaviors, especially when they are consistent with their past behaviors.
5. **Language:** People's ability to communicate in a way that is nonjudgmental, validating, selfless, deep, and focused on you.
6. **Stability:** People's degree of emotional maturity, dependability, and consistency is free from manipulative, self-destructive traits.

PART II

THE SIX SIGNS FOR BEHAVIOR PREDICTION

(How to Size People Up)

3

BUILD BULLETPROOF ALLIANCES

Sign #1: VESTING

Does this person believe they will benefit from your success?

March 18, 2002, 9:00 a.m.
March Madness

"Yeah?"

That's how Leo's grandson answered the phone. His voice was flat with disinterest, so I knew he had seen it was me on the caller ID.

"Hi, Viktor. Is your grandfather around?"

"Yeah." Silence.

The kid—still a stalwart Russian—hated me, even though I'd helped him with his visa and his medical treatment.

Viktor knew enough about my operations to halt my fledgling career in its tracks, but I wasn't at all worried, because that wouldn't be in his best interests. Viktor's grandfather was fully vested in me and my success—as I was in him—and that put Viktor in a very transparent position: If he messed with me, he'd be messing with his grandfather, whom he not only feared but loved far more.

So I was optimistic that Viktor would eventually warm up to me, as strangers often do when they feel like they're in a long-term relationship.

Some people might see that type of advantage as leverage, manipulation, or even emotional blackmail, but to me it was trust. The three of us, like it or not, were jammed into this horrible moment of history together, so we all knew what the others would do.

"How's your treatment going?" I asked.

"I dunno."

"Mine's going okay," I volunteered. We were both being treated for pulmonary toxicity and chronic coughs, caused by inhaling the toxic fumes of Ground Zero.

Looking back, I think the treatment might have saved my life. In the months since 9/11, approximately a thousand more people had already died, many of them due to serious injuries, organ failure, pneumonia, and suicide—including a colleague of mine. Far more were sick or suffering, and soon would die.

Helping Viktor had cemented my relationship with Leo, but Viktor—who hated being an emigrant, and wasn't sold on the American Dream—still saw me as an ambitious, ruthless punk who had turned his grandfather into a traitor. From Viktor's perspective, that made sense to me.

Even back then, I'd learned how to strategically shut down my own point of view when I needed to, and to see myself with the same contempt as the people who didn't like me. It's a painful exercise in self-awareness, but if you can summon enough ego suspension and inner security to view yourself through the eyes of others, it gives you virtual X-ray vision into them.

You can understand why they feel the way they do, and it tells you what they need from you. Often as not, though, it's something you thought you were already giving them. But it's not *your* perspective that matters. It's theirs.

When you get into their heads, you can also see what they consider to be in their own best interests—and when you know that, you can usually predict what they'll do.

"My *friend*!" Leo was on the line. "How can I help you?" His voice sounded much different than it had at our first painful meeting. The Queens influence on his accent seemed to be gone, replaced by a warm, deep tone that was softened even further by his pleasant Russian accent.

Why the difference? Maybe it was because he was prone to compartmentalization, a subconscious psychological defense mechanism many people use to protect themselves from addressing painful emotions. It is often revealed by language patterns, word choices, and tone.

More simply, maybe he just presented himself as a badass Russian New Yorker until he got to know people.

In any case, he sounded like he was smiling—always a great tell, even if I couldn't visually confirm it.

When you're sizing people up, your *greatest sources of information will usually be through conversation.* Conversation provides vocabulary tells, speech tells, nonverbal tells from the rest of the body, and factual information. It often generates a wealth of data points, even on a landline phone call with no visuals. It's even more productive if you get some face time with them, because people are social animals, and because most of us know at least enough about nonverbal communication to have a good idea about how someone feels.

Alternately, though, you can sometimes inspire people to be more straightforward and candid when they know they're not being observed. It's all a matter of collecting data points and going with what seems to work best.

Leo talked for a few more minutes, and then I had to get down to "busy-ness."

"Leo, we're in a world of crap," I said. "State just expelled sixty Russian diplomats, and some of them are *our* guys." Meaning: people he and I relied on as unwitting sources of information—his targets, which he'd passed on to me.

"Because of Hanssen?" He was talking about Robert Hanssen, an FBI agent who was awaiting sentencing for selling secrets to Russia.

"Yes, Hanssen—so now we've got to rebuild our network. At the worst possible time."

Within the Bureau, most of us were pissed about the State Department's mass expulsions of Russian diplomats. We called it March Madness. It had taken Leo decades, in some cases, to build the rapport with these sources. The only reason I didn't feel totally overwhelmed was because agents are trained—in somewhat the same way that I'm training you now—to refrain from solving problems until they're certain that the problems actually exist. But this had certainly knocked me off my stride.

"Meet me at the club?" Leo said. He meant his social club for Russian men, which he operated partly for profit and partly to find new contacts.

"Can we do it after five thirty? I'm on a damage control deadline with my Jedi Master." He knew who I meant: Jesse. "We just got tasked with supporting the Hanssen investigation, going back to his early days in New York."

I knew that Leo hated to desecrate the Happy Hour with business, but he was always great about fulfilling my agenda, on my schedule, as if he had none of his own.

"Five thirty is perfect!" he said.

"It's not gonna be easy to rebuild our network," I said.

"No," he said, with an edgy tone of desperation that was common after 9/11. "But we've *got* to. You and me."

At this point, I didn't know that behavioral analysts considered vesting in other people's interests to be a cornerstone of trust. I just knew how good it felt when he reiterated his commitment to our relationship.

"I know a guy who may be willing to help," Leo said. "We'll start with him and go friend to friend."

That was beyond risky, because it required a tremendous degree of trust for an agent to place their career—and maybe even life—in the hands of someone who starts as a stranger. It's also risky for U.S. national security.

But I eventually ended up taking Leo's audacious advice—mostly out of my own desperation—and its brilliance gave me an education equal to a doctoral dissertation.

Methods in the Madness

I secured my office and bounded up five flights of stairs, just to burn off stress, to the twenty-fifth floor, where Jesse was already half buried in documents about Hanssen. Jesse had worked with Hanssen on a Russian squad for several years, so he and I were expected to come up with something scintillating—in the next nine hours—that would help establish Hanssen's possible earlier ties to the Russians.

"Check it out," Jesse said when I came in. He took a quarter out of his pocket, stood it on the floor, and watched it roll rapidly to the center of the room, which was sagging dangerously from an extraordinary tonnage of paper-heavy files, and was scheduled for a rebuild. The mountain of files was finally being digitized, as the FBI entered the era of big data, with its promise of providing *much better security* for confidential information. Sound ironic?

Jesse watched his quarter gain speed, hit a hill on the other side of the room, come to a halt, and fall. "Know what that shows me?" he said.

I was expecting another life lesson.

"Too damn much paperwork," he said.

Although Jesse was one of the most decorated people in the agency, with sophisticated counterintelligence—or CI—operations on three continents, he relied far more on his relationships than on written records. I didn't have a seasoned network, so I was trying to codify his basic methods for turning personal data points into a system. I love systems, because they can be taught in dirt-simple manuals—along the lines of *Counterintelligence for Dummies* (for people like me). At this point in my life, I've seen systems change the cultures of companies, and even countries.

I also value the power of systems for translating emotion into logic, and eliminating emotion for emotion's sake. Everybody has emotions, but in serious matters, such as counterintelligence, feelings that stray from logic can be deadly. It's too easy to get emotionally hijacked, fly off the handle, and create a mess you can't clean up.

"Look at this one," Jesse said, handing me an article about Hanssen. Notes had been scribbled onto it after his arrest a few weeks earlier, when he'd received a dead drop of $50,000 as part of the $1.4 million in cash and diamonds that Russia had paid him.

For that sum, Hanssen had exposed nine U.S. double agents to Russia's version of the FBI. Three of the agents had been executed, after interrogations that were probably painful. He had also sold Russia information about U.S. nuclear war preparations, as well as surveillance detection technologies that a Russian agent had passed on to Osama bin Laden.

I scanned the dossier. It showed Hanssen's numerous marital indiscretions and his dire need for his father's approval.

I asked Jesse if he'd written anything for our memo about Hanssen's possible earlier work with the Russians.

"No, but I got it up here," he said, tapping his head.

That was good enough for me.

"All I know is what I see," Jesse said, "but that's plenty, if you keep your eyes open. Bottom line on Hanssen: self-involved, paranoid prick. The entire time I worked with him, he never partnered with anybody. Hell, he even ate his lunch alone. No ties. No loyalty. Not even with people who tried to be his friend. He *acted* like he didn't fit in, so of course he didn't. Bob didn't give a rat's ass about anybody but Bob—and he wasn't afraid to say it, because he thought it made him look like an up-and-comer. He was always pissed off about something, always felt persecuted, and acted like he was smarter than the other people on our squad. So we never knew what he was up to. When somebody is paranoid like that, you get paranoid about *them*."

"He turned traitor over hurt feelings?"

"When people are too lazy—or too damaged—to think, they take everything personally, and it messes with their heads."

Jesse handed me an old case file that had been written by Hanssen. It had his supervisor's comments on it, in big red letters: "THIS IS BULLSHIT!!" and "HOW DO YOU KNOW *THIS??*"

"That's typical Bob," Jesse said. "Even his supervisor didn't trust him. But nobody said anything. Ever."

"Why? Or more to the point, why didn't *you*?" Some people would have taken that as an insult. Jesse took it as a question.

"The usual reasons. Benefit of the doubt. Don't rock the boat. Groupthink. 'Everybody else tolerates him, so he must be okay.' And when he finally got to be a supervisor, it got ten times easier for him to be an asshole, as it always does. But Hanssen wasn't some kind of superspy. He was just good at covering his ass."

His face clouded, and he said, "When I was new here—like you are—I wish somebody had taken me aside and said, 'An FBI agent doesn't give people the benefit of the doubt.'"

I'd never heard anyone say that. And it went against the grain of my sense of goodness. Jesse read the doubt in my face.

"An agent makes people *earn* it," he continued. "By collecting information about them—no matter who they are—and by making informed decisions."

I'll be honest—it seemed cynical. He looked at me in a quizzical way that made me feel exposed—he was probably reading my nonverbals—and said, "You don't want to hear that, do you? You like to trust people."

"Doesn't everybody?"

"Not anymore. At least not in this country."

With that sad reference to our post-9/11 new world disorder, we wrote up what we'd discovered in the archives.

I was flipping from being a wide-eyed innocent—just one step removed from the flower-power philosophies of the 1970s—to being somebody who, hopefully, would soon deserve the trust of his colleagues and country.

I was also learning some of that perspective from the people in our Washington field office who were leading the Hanssen investigation. From those lessons, and others that followed, I now know this: It's wise to trust everybody—until they start talking, which is usually right away. At that point, if you're interested in doing something important with them, you've got to start thinking like an FBI behavioral analyst: rationally, carefully, and objectively. You have to see people for who they *are*, with your vision unclouded by fear, affection, or just plain laziness.

If they say the right things, do the right the things, and show the right intentions, keep trusting them.

Some of them will become people that you trust with your life.

Most won't. But that's okay, because it's not their purpose on earth to be the trustee of your life. Their life is about them, just as yours is about you, and they apparently don't think that having you in their life will make much difference. You just need to figure out—with *facts*—where they're headed. And if they're not headed the same place you are, so be it.

At that point, you can still trust them to do what's in their own best interests, and they can easily remain an ally, even if they become a competitor. That happens all the time, and with enough humility and rationality, you can build a relationship with a competitor that lasts far longer than any temporary competition you might have had with them. So stay flexible. I learned that in the marines. One of our mottoes was *Semper Gumby*.

The reality is, very few people are looking to hurt you. They're just trying to take care of themselves and their families—as you are—so it's against your best interests to judge them for that. If you do, you'll ruin any future chance for mutual vesting, because people can smell a judgmental attitude a mile away.

Over time, people and situations change—and someone who pushed you away in the past may want to vest in you. That's always exciting, because vesting is an excellent creator and barometer of affiliation. When someone decides that your success is their success, they're powerfully motivated to do whatever they can for you. In your professional life, vesting is the ultimate animator of teamwork, and at home, it's what keeps a family near and dear.

I usually experience vesting in only about one-fifth of the people who seem to share some or all of my goals. Many of the other 80 percent are reluctant to offer trust because they've been burned. You can look at that reticence to vest as a negative, but you can also see it as a sign of someone's intelligence and sincerity. Trust is sacred. It shouldn't be squandered, and it carries obligations for those who take it seriously.

Many people tiptoe into trust, which is usually smart. But occasionally the tells of willingness to vest—expressed in words, deeds, and intentions—are so obvious that it results in a phenomenon I call "trust at first sight."

The Negative Tells for Vesting

Each of the tells of trust—also referred to here as "negative tells"—and distrust will be conveyed to you in the following four ways:

Verbal communication: What they say, and how they say it.

Nonverbal communication: Body language that either confirms their message, or causes you to doubt it.

Actions: Current and past actions that are recorded in public and private sources of information.

Intentions: Stated and/or observed, that indicate someone's relative degree of alignment with your own goals and dreams.

The tells of distrust are often less significant than the tells of trust, mostly because they are more ambiguous and open to interpretation.

A tell of distrust may stem from simple lack of interest in you, or from a benign misunderstanding.

To understand the tells of vesting, we'll start with the ones that indicate that someone is *not* willing to vest in you. These tells are usually hard to miss, simply because they hurt.

The tells of distrust described here are very common, but there are countless variations. These will give you an excellent idea, though, of the content and tone of many other tells, some of which may apply to you alone, since we're all different people, in different situations.

Warning: When these very common tells of distrust occur, don't assume the worst. The tells of distrust can be tricky, and it's easy to get emotionally hijacked.

Stay rational and don't take things personally until you get the facts.

Even if the facts show that someone does not want to vest in you, you should still try to make the best of the situation. Try to solve the problem, and if you can't, move on—and embrace the change.

Learning how to embrace every situation in a positive way can be life-changing. In the science of behavioral analysis—unlike the hard sciences of math or physics—a positive attitude, applied wisely and vigorously, can transform almost anything into a positive.

TEN NEGATIVE TELLS FOR VESTING IN YOUR SUCCESS

1. Supervisors pass you over for a promotion and give it to someone with whom you work. This is often the strongest negative tell, because it clearly shows that you're not perceived as the person who will best enhance the life of the supervisor who awarded the promotion.

The first time can mean nothing. Several times sends a clear message: Start being more helpful to others—especially your bosses—or look for a new job.

Maybe, though, they're just looking for something better to give you.

2. Your bosses point out ways that you're different from them. Ouch! Opposites don't attract—they repel.

Your supervisors are saying: You'll never be part of our tribe until you start making our lives better. If you don't, you're dispensable.

It's a clear warning. Ask, in a sincere way, how you can make your supervisors' lives better.

If it's something you can live with, give it a try. If it's not, stay classy and try to depart in your own time and your own style.

3. Your bosses leave you out of meetings that your peers attend. This is also one of the worst tells. It's obvious that they think you're not needed, probably because you're not doing your best to help other people do *their* best.

But don't assume the obvious. When I was young, I often made an issue out of this, but that just made things worse. Maybe you don't belong in the meeting—so figure out where you *do* belong, and work your way up from there with actions that include helping your supervisors and peers to succeed.

People usually won't leave you out of a meeting if they think you'll help them push their own agenda.

4. People with power over you exaggerate the importance of your trivial errors. They're probably trying to find reasons to get rid of you, most likely because they don't think their own careers are benefiting from your presence.

In many companies, people's careers are often linked to the performance of their division, or the company as a whole, so their sense of their own best interests can extend to the company itself.

When you are helping others and helping your company, people find ways to downplay errors.

So get the facts—straight from the person who criticizes you—and let the facts, rather than your fear, guide your response.

5. Your immediate supervisor mentions other departments where you might excel. If you hear it from a supervisor who shows no *other* signs of being vested in your success, it usually means you're not giving them what they want. You'd better start—right away. They seem to think they'd be better off without you.

But if it's from someone who does show signs of being vested in you, jump at it. Tell them your dreams.

Either way, stay positive. People who look for the worst usually find it, often creating disaster out of thin air.

6. Executives engage in negative nonverbals while you're offering your ideas. This tell is critically important, because someone's nonverbals are often more revealing than what they say.

The easiest negative nonverbals to notice include eyelid flutters, lip compression, eyebrow furrowing, or a failure to look you in the eye, shake your hand, or smile at you. As a rule, I look at people's facial expressions more than any other form of nonverbal behavior, because faces are the most revealing.

Most of these nonverbal tells say: I don't want to hear another word, because I don't think it's going to help me get what I need right now.

7. Your boss asks you about rumors that you've done something wrong. This is a bad tell, without much wiggle room. Regardless of the veracity of the rumor, it's bad management to listen to rumors and then hit somebody over the head with them. It's very passive-aggressive.

But if it comes from someone who considers you very valuable to them, thank them for the warning.

8. Your organization's decision makers text or email while they're talking to you, or walk away while you're still talking. Unless this occurs in the middle of a crisis, both are tells that your career doesn't matter to them.

Someone walking away while you're talking is the worst. It's blatant—and if they do it in front of others, it's the kiss of death. They clearly don't think you're valuable to them.

If this happens repeatedly and pointedly, accept the information, deal with it rationally, and get ready to leave—or make yourself *much* more valuable while you still have time.

9. Leaders never say, "I really want you to succeed here," or words to that effect. What doesn't get said is often as important as what does. How much clearer can it be? They don't really care.

Suck it up and initiate the issue: "I want to contribute to your success and the company's. What suggestions do you have on how I can be a better resource?"

If you do validate their criticism, you'll feel vulnerable, right? Don't worry about it. You were already vulnerable.

10. People challenge your thoughts and opinions. Most people are sure that this is a bad sign—because it often is. But good leaders and valuable peers typically challenge the ideas of the people they value most, because they take their ideas seriously.

The worst-case scenario is that they feel critical of you, even more than any individual thought or opinion you offer. They're just looking for a peg where they can hang their hater-hat.

So assess the criticism for validity, importance, and its mode of presentation. Some leaders *like* a dialogue that's based on differences of opinion.

If they've got a good point, thank them for their input—sincerely, not passive-aggressively—and jump on it. Working for people means working on their behalf.

Now ask yourself: How many of these following tells apply to you? Are you doing enough research before you decide something? Have you ever gotten burned by someone who went quickly in and out of your life? Have other people misled you when you didn't have time to check on what they said?

These are the types of questions that you need to ask yourself after each of the tells—positive and negative—for the rest of the book. But I won't waste your time by mentioning it again.

March 18, 2002, 5:30 p.m.
The Outsiders

I arrived a few minutes early for my meeting with Leo at a place called the Outsiders Club, the social hall he owned. It was part of his outdoor adventure company—for guided events such as hunting, fishing, or hiking—that was used by Russian tourists or businesspeople, as well as for Leo's own clique of Russian emigrants.

The name had a double meaning that the guests from abroad were not privy to. "Outsiders" did not refer solely to outdoorsmen—as the visitors usually presumed, for obvious reasons. It also referred to the antipathy of the local emigrants, almost all of whom were alienated from Russia. Some of them worked as confidential human sources, under Leo's wing. Almost all of them came from the former satellite nations controlled by the Soviet Union—including Ukraine, Georgia, and the -stan states like Uzbekistan or Kazakhstan. Those were the hot spots that were already locked in a bloody state of perma-rebellion against Russia and its new president, the former failed KGB agent Vladimir Putin, who somehow managed to land on his feet after his poor performance as an agent.

The importance of knowing details applied even more stringently to Leo's visitors from Russia, who were often intelligence officers (aka spies) and were obviously unaware that Leo was a double agent. They had an ugly streak of entitlement that stemmed from being upper-crust residents of the Moscow area, or Muscovites, who were also known as White Russians. The "white" delineated them from the "ethnic" Russians of the breakaway states. Ethnic Russians had long been second-class citizens in their own society, even during the "classless" Soviet era. No ethnic Russian, here or in the motherland, had ever been an agent for the KGB or its new incarnation, the SVR. Nor were there any female SVR agents at this time, because they were not considered—believe it or not—intelligent enough for the position.

If these bizarre differentiations that govern Russian trust seem like arcane and archaic leftovers from a long-ago tribal past, remember that tribal warfare has been the most enduring of all human conflicts and still dominates the world's modern military engagements. It's been going on for centuries, and involves people with whom I have worked.

Some of these people were very vulnerable to severe retribution then—and some may still be. In the world of counterintelligence, people's lives and reputations are always on the line, and discretion and confidentiality are always at play. That's why I don't use real names in these anecdotes, and change details that would expose people to harm.

America is vastly less punitive to innocent people, but it also has many divisions. In America, tribal trust is currently dominated by the smoldering, divisive differences of race, money, religion, and politics, and try as we might to have a reasonable rationale, many of us hand out trust like candy to anybody in our own tribe. But that's very unwise.

The irrationality of trust even infects America in its most supposedly rational institutions, including national security. For example, a flirty and attractive female cyberthreat analyst recently made connections with hundreds of people—82 percent males—from the U.S. military, intelligence agencies, and information security companies. Google and Lockheed Martin expressed interest in hiring her, and she was offered speaking engagements at security conferences. But the "woman" was just an avatar created by a national security researcher to see how gullible people—especially men—can be when they don't look beyond a pretty face.

I was on a team that had a somewhat similar experience with a genuine Russian spy, Anna Chapman, who used her charm and beauty to hack American security.

So I had no illusions, as I waited for Leo to arrive, about the vulnerability to manipulation in assessing people that we *all* share—especially in a crisis, when we are most in need of the ability to accurately size people up.

At this moment, though, I was indeed in a crisis. I needed to quickly rebuild a team of informants—both witting and unwitting.

When Leo, the club president, burst through the door with his husky Lion King build and bighearted smile, the differences in the room seemed to diminish. But not among everyone. Many of the men were still very Russian, and the cultural norm in Russia is that people who smile effusively are less trustworthy.

"Hello, men!" Leo boomed.

He gave me a big hug and waved for two glasses of what had become our traditional drink: Gzhelka White Gold vodka. "I love this," Leo said, lowering his voice to a conspiratorial decibel, which felt appropriate, considering my misgivings about what he had in mind. "Starting new operations! Rebuilding the team! Learning from you! I dreamed of days like this in the camps, just to stay alive—and it's happening!"

He touched his glass to mine, with shiny eyes. "Thank you for this dream, my good friend."

I touched his glass. His appreciation was contagious—as that trait always is—and his pride in our work was inspiring.

But after fourteen prior handlers, why did Leo trust me? I had to assume it started when I offered to help him. Nothing else made sense.

"How is Valentina?" I asked. He'd recently gotten remarried, and three days later his wife had been in a car wreck.

"My Valentine is not well. Medicare issues." His eyes went dry, a sign that he was back into survival mode.

"What can I do for you?"

"A word to the right person in the Bronx division of Social Security?"

"I will do everything I can." That was—thank God—something I could do. My neighbor worked for the Social Security Administration. Jesse had long ago advised me to form great relationships with *everyone* in my life. You never know . . .

Leo leaned close. "Your priority now is terrorism," he said, his voice now a husky whisper. "I have worked with you only on Russian issues.

I have another idea, if you will indulge me." His eyes were wide and searching.

"Only if it can be good for *you*, too," I said.

He bent even closer. "I grew up with a man who lives in Manhattan now named Sergei. And my father—he was a country doctor, you know?"

"I do know."

"My father saved the life of Sergei's sister, and on that day Sergei pledged to me that I was his"—he had to take a breath—"brother for life. For *life*." He said the word with reverence, having seen so much life casually destroyed. "Sergei works at the Russian consulate now, but he is not a White Russian. So for him diplomacy is a difficult business." As earlier in our relationship, he pronounced it *busy-ness*—probably on purpose. He always became more Russian when he was near Russians.

"Is he a member of the club?" I asked.

"The Outsiders?" Leo asked softly. "Or the other?" He meant the clandestine services.

"The Outsiders. This place."

"Yes, the Outsiders only," he said. "He is a clean diplomat." That meant he was not with Special Services—the spy network—and would not be on anybody's radar, ours or theirs.

"He loves Russia. In the way some men love wives who do not deserve it. But he loves me more. As one should." Leo cherished his adopted country of America enough to do things that could get him quietly assassinated, but he held the love for people as the most sacred of all.

"Then why would he talk to me?"

"Because he loves me. And I love you." He said it in a matter-of-fact way, but it still put a lump in my throat.

"I'd be happy to meet him." I didn't have the heart to say it, but this did *not* sound wise.

Leo reached over, shook my hand, and let it linger. Two more drinks suddenly appeared, and I handed one to him.

"*Nostrovia!*" I said, clinking his glass.

I thought about how distant and despairing he'd been only seven months earlier—when I still had the acrid stink of Ground Zero on my clothing—and I felt a sense of wonder for the finest feature of the human spirit: the generosity that lies deep within it, anxious to emerge.

I also knew—despite this moment, which touched me to my core—that America, Leo, his wife, Viktor, myself, and the huge grieving city of New York were still in a world of pain and chaos. We were all refugees, in our own way, from a new kind of war that threatened never to end—and never has.

I just hoped that Leo's friend Sergei wouldn't report me to a security officer, who would probably make a protest to the U.S. State Department and create a big diplomatic mess—with me at the center.

It could easily turn into an international incident at a time of serious national vulnerability. It was also possible that the Russians would punish me personally. I'd be largely immune if I stayed in the States, but if I traveled abroad, it might be quite different.

Leo and some of the other Outsiders I had met here were familiar with a far darker and more dangerous life than the one I had led, and I could see how something as dicey as approaching a known Russian loyalist would seem reasonable to them.

I knew I needed to find a dependable, systematic method that would enable me to succeed in this bizarre business—or at least to survive. But I didn't know where to start, other than with what I later learned was the most important aspect of sizing somebody up: vesting in Leo's success, by continuing to help his grandson.

Even though the kid was a loose cannon, I knew I was doing the right thing.

March 21, 2002
Staying Positive

I spent the next few days picking Jesse's brain about how to deal with the Sergei situation, and he was even more optimistic than usual. He'd seen the deadly side of war and espionage, and was hard to rattle. Even by 2002, though, I'd learned enough from Jesse and Leo to consider having a *very frank* discussion with Sergei, if I saw the tells of vesting that I needed. Why not? If I think that your success is my success, why wouldn't I trust you?

Over the years, in almost all of the cases that included vesting, the relationships and objectives succeeded—especially in the business world, since it revolves around money, which is easy to measure.

A company is more likely to succeed over the long term if:

- **Owners and C-suite executives** believe that, for them to succeed, they need to vest in the success of their direct reports.
- **Managers** believe that, to succeed, they need to vest in their employees.
- **Investors** believe that management is primarily looking out for them.
- **Customers** believe that the company is driven by customer satisfaction.

In personal relationships, though, vesting is probably even more powerful. Among the happy couples I know, each person not only loves the other, but is convinced that anything that happens to their partner—good or bad—affects them equally.

The following ten tells are very common and carry a lot of clout. But use them partly to notice tells of your own.

TEN POSITIVE TELLS FOR VESTING IN YOUR SUCCESS

1. People are happy to work at your tempo, and in your work style instead of theirs. There are people who just won't allow others to disrupt their way of doing things, and they tend not to vest in others simply because we all have somewhat different ways of getting things done.

People who are comfortable vesting in others, though, are

proud of bending over backward to accommodate the needs of their close associates.

2. People typically talk in terms of your own priorities, interests, and prosperity. They make you the center of attention because they see you as their surrogate and don't need to recapture the spotlight for themselves. The wise response is to grant them the same courtesy and commitment.

3. People look for ways to expand their relationship with you. They seek further common interests, and include you in many of the important things they do, even if it's not something you can do on a level equal to theirs. They'll find a way to employ your skills.

They will also bridge the gap between personal and professional relationships—by bringing you into their personal life if you work together, or by sharing their professional life with you if they're a social friend.

4. People join you in a difficult project even when they would rather not. On several occasions, colleagues of mine have been assigned to something that felt like a death march to me, but I've volunteered to join them out of personal consideration. There's no better foundation for vesting than to suck it up and dive in.

A less dramatic but still meaningful way to show you're vested in someone's success is to work unpaid overtime with them, especially if you can contribute something they can't.

As always, actions speak loudest. That's partly why I volunteer as a pilot for a medical airlift organization. It's time and resource intensive, and is the most action-oriented contribution I can make.

5. People call in their own favors on your behalf. Cashing in the currency held in someone's own "favor bank" is a huge tell of vesting. It not only signals the proactive willingness of their help, but also often creates a new relationship for you, if you meet the person who owed the favor.

It can also create what's called the Benjamin Franklin Effect: When someone does a favor for you, it makes them like you more, because they've invested in you and would suffer from cognitive dissonance if they didn't like you. It's almost pure elixir of vesting. Franklin discovered it when he borrowed a book from an enemy and found that the guy no longer disliked him.

6. Virtually all of someone's positive actions are unsolicited. I call this the "initiative test." If someone helps you on their own initiative, it indicates much more vesting than if you have to ask them for help.

It shows even more vesting if they create new forums, tasks, or venues that are intended to help you, such as forming a committee and putting you at its head.

7. People create a positive image of you inside and outside of your company, and give you credit for success that they were involved with, at the expense of their own credit. This form of self-branding not only connotes faith in their connection with you, but also reveals the generosity and emotional stability of their own personality.

If this extremely valuable tell comes from an immediate supervisor, it shows that they care enough about you to risk the chance of losing you to another company or division—or even to run the risk of you taking their own job.

People who consistently create a positive brand for you are pure gold. Treat them well and the mutual trust will run deep.

8. People show genuine excitement about your achievements. That's usually because they see your success as theirs, too, but it can also indicate pure generosity. If they don't show excitement, but seem to be guardedly resentful or jealous, you may want to find another ally.

It's even better if they show unabashed pleasure at the prospect of benefiting from your achievement. In that case, there's nothing shameful about somebody benefiting from you and voicing it.

9. People extend their professional relationship with you into a social one. This is huge and also very common. The bilevel connection creates two separate, mutually reinforcing forms of commitment. It also indicates that they enjoy you as a person, and not just someone who can help them.

10. People tell you something they've never told anyone else. This is huge!

They trust your discretion and advice, and see you as nonjudgmental.

Of those values, the one I admire most is the refusal to judge, which strongly encourages the people around you to be honest. It also creates a relaxed, congenial atmosphere.

When someone opens their heart to you, you can't help but see yourself in a better light. It quiets your self-criticism, and helps you rise above being your own best enemy.

March 30, 2002
Trust at First Sight

"It's a go," my supervisor said. "HQ authorized the contact."

I'd had to go through channels on the Sergei operation and was glad that my meeting with him had been approved. But it was not unanimous: Some people were fiercely opposed.

I didn't like my odds and I hated the timing. Gaining the cooperation of a diplomat is as likely as winning the lottery—which is why we often referred to this scenario as "hitting lotto."

The biggest risk was that Sergei would rat me out to his embassy, because diplomats can get an instant promotion for reporting such contact to their security officers. And the time crunch mandated a one-meeting agreement instead of, say, two years—which is about average and is safer.

So lacking anything tangible to offer, I'd have to extend what I call trust at first sight: genuine, respectful consideration for the other person's best interests.

These days, I can confidently offer my own trust to almost anyone—until they abuse it, which happens—but back then I didn't realize how flexible I could be with trust. I was still hooked on the notion—which seems quaint now—that trust was a spiritual and moral absolute that could never be retracted, or even modified. The very idea that you could love someone and still not trust them remained foreign to me.

I was concerned, though, that Sergei would feel constrained by the power of his government. For well over a hundred years, Russians have generally been dominated by strong governments: starting with the czars, then the Soviet commissars, and then the drug czars in Putin's billionaire boys club.

I called Sergei at a covert number provided by Leo, and he agreed to meet me at a Wall Street restaurant called Reserve Cut. My dining choice was an unspoken message to him that nobody in his consulate would see him in lower Manhattan, miles from its location on the Upper East Side.

He agreed immediately. Most Russian diplomats would have insisted I visit them at their office, indicating very politely that they didn't even want to consider the possibility of an "unofficial relationship." Maybe Sergei just wanted to get away from his grim, gray consulate and eat at a spendy, trendy in-spot. Leo had told me that Sergei didn't get out much and always appreciated a good meal with friendly conversation.

On D-Day, as the maître d' led Sergei to my table, I made a baseline read of his body language: eyebrows tensed with compression, lips tight, head tilted back in reticence, arms folded in front of him. He eyeballed me, too, as he read my body for the same information. A quick, soft handshake. Shields up. He glanced at his watch. Bad sign.

"Sergei, thank you so much for taking the time to have a conversation with me. Although I wish our mutual good friend had been able to make it." No reason to name names.

I'd talked to Leo about having him join us, as a way to help put Sergei at ease, but we decided it might actually inhibit Sergei, if he and I actually did get down to a deal.

The mention of Leo softened Sergei's face slightly as he scanned the room of power brokers approvingly—as Leo thought he would—without seeming self-conscious. His suit and shirt didn't meet the implicit dress code, but he wore them well. He had broad shoulders and a trim physique, and looked better than most of his Russian counterparts, who tended to be pale and pudgy from their numbing number of office hours.

"Our friend thought we had a few things in common and might be able to find other common interests, with commensurate resources," I said.

Sergei looked relieved that I'd immediately acknowledged the reality of the situation—in the bonding, ambiguous international language of bureaucracy—instead of insulting his intelligence with head games. In his relief, a few more lines left his face.

His response encouraged me enough to offer him another taste of reality, although I would again need to shade it in vague language, to acknowledge the gravity of my statement, and to give him room for denial if things went south.

"I know you're a diplomat," I said, "but let's say, hypothetically, that somebody in your consulate was in Special Services." His brows raised slightly, because that was code for intel. It was also a tacit admission that I, too, was in "special services"—the term used by real-life spies, who almost never say "spy." The corners of his mouth canted slightly upward: a subtle signal of assent. We already had a grain of mutual vesting!

But as he sipped a drink and fussed with his napkin, he glanced at his watch again—which might have been a brush-off, so I asked him point-blank if he needed to be somewhere. At the very least, it would show my sensitivity to his needs. But if he said he had to leave soon, it would mean: *No dice. Game over.* Let's order!

"Not at all," he said. "I have as long as you'd like." Good sign! He wasn't actually withdrawing, but simply had some time constraints, and was subordinating his schedule to mine. (That's Positive Tell #1. I'll keep pointing out the positive tells. I'm sure you've already noticed some of the negative tells, such as his unmistakably negative nonverbals.)

I asked him how he'd met Leo, as an open-ended "inkblot" test to see where he'd go. If he gave me an abrupt "That was long ago," he'd be saying that his relationship with Leo was none of my business—and that I had no hope of piggybacking on Leo's relationship with him.

This might seem like nothing but small talk, but I've found that all talk can be important and significant, if it enables you to build a healthy, mutually supportive relationship.

I've also found that, as a rule, the further people go back in their lives, the more they lower their shields, presumably because of some primal instinct.

Here are other tells of vesting I was looking for: Is he appropriately receptive to neutral subjects? Is he proactive about revealing himself? Is he willing to share something that's important to him? Will he say something he hasn't told anyone else? Is he going to hand me a couple of nuggets that promised more?

As I'd requested before Sergei arrived, the waiter brought two glasses of top-shelf Gzhelka White Gold vodka, which was not only Leo's favorite, but also Sergei's. That was another way to show Sergei that Leo had told me several things about him (hopefully without it seeming creepy), and it increased the level of intimacy between Sergei and me—whether he liked it or not. It was a complicated encounter, but probably no more complex than the hard meetings in your profession. Manipulation, deceit, and temptation are everywhere.

So Sergei gradually surrendered the false presumption of enjoying full privacy and told me about the day Leo's father had saved his sister's life. His memories triggered emotion, but he controlled it well, and again we crossed a bridge of connection.

Then I asked him another open-ended question, making it sound as spontaneous as possible. "What was your favorite childhood holiday or tradition?" It's my all-time favorite, and has evoked many fascinating and enriching reactions, because it's a nonthreatening way to break the ice with people and help shift their mood to one of receptivity. It brings them back to a time and place where they felt happy and safe, and ratchets up the contentment neurotransmitters of dopamine and serotonin—though not quite as effectively as good vodka, which they served generously here, as I'd arranged. He told me what a Russian Orthodox Christmas was like, as he settled into an amazing tuna and white truffle appetizer.

"Robin," he said. "What are you looking for? Why are we chatting?" Great! It was the first tell indicating that he wanted to share more than a two-hundred-dollar lunch with me. And it was unsolicited (Positive Tell #6)!

"I'd like to get an understanding of your priorities and interests," I said, "to see if I could be a resource for any of them."

He nodded amiably. "What are *your* priorities?" he asked. Nice! He was shifting the focus to me (Positive Tell #2). I was warming up to him!

"Right now I'm rebuilding, in the aftermath of the Robert Hanssen case."

"That sounds important!" He pumped me for more details—taking pains to show me he wasn't looking for anything classified—and seemed genuinely impressed that I was working at that level so early in my career (Positive Tell #8).

I brought the conversation back to our very different childhoods—not for business purposes, but because it's my nature to be curious. To connect, you've got to be yourself, win or lose, because people are extremely well attuned to manipulation these days. Any whiff of it can make them go cold in a heartbeat.

After another vodka, I asked, "So what do you think we might be able to do together? Something both our countries would be happy about?" I liked the guy. He was a straight shooter and smart—everything Leo claimed. "What are *your* interests?"

"To make the world better for my children. *Safer,*" he said pointedly. That kind of goody-goody response can be canned and insincere, but he continued: "I sometimes take them . . . took them . . . to lower Manhattan, around the World Trade Center." He stopped abruptly. Russian spies don't show sentiment, and merely mentioning his kids— in the same sentence as the WTC—had obviously touched a chord.

"When the airplanes hit," he said, "I wasn't sure where my children were, or what would happen next." His face was stoic, but he again stopped abruptly.

To fill the silence, I said, "I understand that. All too well."

"Fathers are fathers everywhere," he said (Positive Tell #9).

"Of course. Our first priority is always their safety."

"Please. . . ." He was hesitant. "I am taking a risk chatting with you, and did it only as a favor to our mutual friend. If you value your relationship with him and wish to continue to chat, this must remain between us. He would understand your discretion, I am sure" (Positive Tell #10).

The tells of trust were coming more quickly. That's usually the norm: Trust invites trust. "I wasn't sure what to expect when I came here," I said, "but I was hopeful, based on the warm feelings our friend holds toward you. And this has exceeded what I had hoped for."

His entrée of salmon and black caviar came, with some tiny, crunchy tempura vegetables. "We should meet again," Sergei said (Positive Tell #3), as he spread some caviar on a toast-point coated with cream and lemon.

"Do you have friends in Special Services back home?" I asked. I didn't think he would answer, and he didn't. But he gave me a half-smile to show that he wasn't offended by my effort—and that, hell yes, of course he did.

That wasn't a nosy spy question, even though it came out like one. Just more curiosity—I like getting to know people. But I was glad he didn't question why I wanted to know. That raised *my* comfort level. So I asked him to name one of his favorite memories as a kid. That's another pacifying, evocative question.

He told me about building a country home, or dacha, with his father. In return, I told him about my family's far more frugal camping trips to a lake. I enjoyed being the only one at the table with a working-class background, and he appreciated the irony.

Then he said, "I cannot help you on many of the things that you may wish I would." I was only mildly disappointed. Even in those days, I knew that building a relationship with an important person is usually more valuable than solving a momentary problem. "But if you are curious about some of my thoughts on terrorism . . . ?" His mind reading reminded me of Jesse.

"Absolutely."

"I can facilitate that interest of yours by calling a person in my home state who is indebted to me. And he can tell you things that will help you, and may be of some service to my own country, and to me as well" (Positive Tell #5). "If a cooperative agreement is reached," he said, "I will stay involved, even though that will be difficult, for several reasons. But that is my problem, not yours. Of course, if you succeed, it will be of great benefit to me" (Positive Tell #4).

Then he dropped an amazing gift onto my lap—even now it is classified information. I can tell you, though, that it involved terrorists who had infiltrated various insurgent militias in his home state, and in other republics that were rebelling against Russia.

An operation against them would be great for American national security. It would limit the geographic spread of al-Qaeda, forcing them to stay centralized and to remain an identifiable, actionable target.

"I will not, of course, tell my people that you and I have had a cordial midday meal," he said. "But perhaps in the future we both will have higher ranks and titles, and perhaps the ties between our countries will strengthen by then, and we can cooperate more openly" (Positive Tell #7).

As you have undoubtedly noticed, this meeting—which produced notable results that probably saved many lives—was not a cloak-and-dagger exercise in mind manipulation, nor was it a lovefest between two people who are dying to please each other. It was just two managers coming together, rationally and respectfully—and seeing signs of personal similarities, and a confluence of interests.

That's all—but that's *everything*.

We ordered dessert and ate it in a comfortable silence, mostly because it was the best dessert that either of us had eaten in a year. We both did, after all, work for the government. Mine was a chocolate cake with hot fudge sauce, perched on miniature cookies and topped with whipped cream. I was too busy with mine to look at his.

The United States made valuable use of Sergei's information. And it brought the two superpowers closer than they'd been in years.

That didn't last. But it showed that it was possible—and that in a rational world, it could happen again.

August 20, 2017
Remembrance

"Sergei!" I said. I hadn't seen him since 2009. We'd stopped chatting after I left New York to follow a close associate of mine to FBI Headquarters in Washington, D.C.

I didn't want to take the position there, but I was mutually vested with my associate, a former supervisor, and that was more important than staying where I was.

It ultimately paid off, in the opportunity to run the Behavioral Analysis Program—although not in the way I thought it would. More on that later.

As a career strategy, some people follow the money and make good friends, while others follow their friends and make good money. Both approaches work, I've found, but the latter provides far more predictability and less worry. You're not always waiting for your house of cards to fall.

"How good it is to see you!" Sergei said, pulling me in for a hug. "But at such a sad time."

We were at the reception that followed Leo's funeral.

Sergei had flown in from Moscow, a touching tribute to our mutual friend.

"I just saw Viktor," I said. "He's taking this hard, but he's as tough as his grandfather, and that will save him." Viktor had given me a beautiful shotgun that Leo had left in his will for me. He'd thanked me for the hundredth time for helping him stay healthy and stay in America, way back in the bad old days of jubilee, when we both learned to trust again. I learned to trust his grandfather, his grandfather learned to trust me, and Leo and I together helped Viktor learn to trust America.

Sergei and I caught up on our kids, wives, and careers, as if no time had passed.

At a funeral, it's easy to see time as humankind's single most shared enemy, since time alone measures age, and age demands decline, which ends in death.

So the specter of loss and a ticking clock haunts every funeral, but even as we say good-bye to those we'll never again see, we inevitably feel the *sweetness* of time, with its gift of growth, and its rich endowment of layer upon layer of memory and meaning.

Remembering Sergei and Leo brought back memories of the time after 9/11, when trust had left my life and I was forced to ask myself why I should ever trust anyone again.

But that's like asking, "Why love?"

By 2017, Russia and America, as personified by our two presidents, were locked at a level of paralytic combat not seen since the Cold War, and that dreadful conflict alone answers the question of "Why trust?" Simple: Because if you do it rationally, it's better than the alternative.

"I'm retiring in two months," Sergei said, as he poured two shots of Gzhelka White Gold. "And I will be working for an international company that you will find interesting." He looked at me appraisingly, bringing back memories of our first meeting.

"Do you want me to call you then?" I asked.

"Yes. There is more work that we can do."

"Until then."

"To our friend!" We clinked glasses, and the bond was born again.

DEBRIEFING

CHAPTER 3:
"BUILD BULLETPROOF ALLIANCES"

SIGN #1: VESTING

Key Quote: "The three of us, like it or not, were jammed into this horrible moment of history together, so we all knew what the others would do."

Key Message: Vesting in the success of another person means openly allying with them, and actively helping them to succeed, based upon the belief that their success will benefit you. Vesting requires courage and brains. It pays off, but only if you play it right.

THE TAKEAWAYS

1. **Vesting is not considered to be a virtuous act,** because making allies is inspired by one's own self-interest. But it can create gratitude and friendship, particularly in a long-term relationship. Vesting in someone is essentially a form of investment.
2. **Vesting is a common practice in business.** It's also present among most immediate family members, and sometimes among friends, especially if the friendship is based partly upon professional ties.

3. Vesting is the single strongest animating force in team-work, professionally and personally.

The Four Main Ways the Tells of Trust and Distrust Are Conveyed:

Verbal communication is the most straightforward means of discovering what people want. And giving people what they want is the best way to build the empowering alliances that are character-ized by the virtues of trust, honesty, and mutual support.

Nonverbal communication, known colloquially as body language, is an effective method of conveying and interpreting what people truly believe, even when it is not consistent with what they are saying.

Actions speak more honestly than words. They are often the most powerful tells of any of the six signs. Past actions are revealing, but current actions—if they benefit both parties—are an even more powerful tell for predicting continued mutual benefit.

Intentions, stated as well as observed, indicate a person's rela-tive degree of alignment with your own goals and dreams.

Ten Positive Tells for Vesting in Your Success

1. They change their work style and tempo to fit yours.
2. They talk in terms of your best interests.
3. They actively explore other things they can do with you.
4. They do things with you that they'd rather not do.
5. They call in their own favors to help you.
6. They offer help even when you don't ask for it.
7. They talk you up inside the company and industry, and give you credit for things they did with you.
8. They get genuinely excited when you succeed.
9. They bring you into their social circle.
10. They share deep secrets.

Ten Negative Tells for Vesting in Your Success

1. They pass you over for a promotion.
2. They mention ways you're different from them.
3. They leave you out of key meetings.
4. They make a big deal out of your small errors.
5. They tell you about other places where you'd do better.
6. When you present ideas, their nonverbals seem purposely negative.
7. They mention an unflattering rumor about you.
8. They look at their devices while you're talking, or walk away.
9. They're much more tight with praise for you than they are with others.
10. They look for negatives in your thoughts and opinions.

MAKE TIME COUNT

Sign #2: LONGEVITY

*Does this person think they will
have a long relationship with you?*

April 2002
Agents Don't Sweat

A perpetual irony of historic upheaval is that it rarely feels historic at the time. The heat of the moment just feels hot. Not like history.

The same general principle applies to heroism. People usually aren't aware of it when they're acting heroically. They're usually too busy, too exhausted, or too frightened.

And too often, heroism is conferred posthumously.

In the clandestine services, there's yet another layer of irony that shrouds incidents of history, heroism, and the cases that create them: Nobody *knows* about them. *Ever.* At least, that's the goal.

That's partly why it's so important to have a reliable system for sizing people up and assuring predictability. Without it, logic and reality can get lost, and not even heroism can make history flow the way we want.

In the cataclysmic months after 9/11, when the world changed radically and time slowed to a crawl, I met a hero who changed history, but it took me years to fully appreciate his contribution. Only the passage of time, I've found, offers the clarity of vision that's generally absent during turbulent times.

My encounter with this man's heroism started on the aircraft carrier *Intrepid*, the temporary site of FBI operations in New York during the shell-shocked period when our tower was being repaired from the World Trade Center attack, about five blocks from us. Every agent in the city was confined to reacting only to 9/11 tips, instead of working any of the usual proactive cases that created new opportunities, attracted new spies, protected America's security, and supported myriad global projects.

The fall of the World Trade Center was the worst thing that could possibly occur—or so it seemed at that time.

So I didn't know what to do when Leo called one morning in the early spring and told me that I needed to meet another member of the Outsiders Club. But the member had nothing to do with 9/11, so I was dubious about seeing him—and didn't even know if I'd be allowed to. Leo sounded unsettled, though, and repeated a very short and explicitly worded message from the guy—the kind of thing that's never put into writing.

The message was essentially a plea for contact with a federal intelligence official, and implied a great deal of urgency, but offered no clear reason for it. This potential CHS was obviously being ultradiscreet, as confidential human sources often are. It ended, Leo said, with a cryptic and indirect plea for help, due to the fact that "we are all mortal." People tend to contact the FBI every time they see Bigfoot flying a UFO—and the days after 9/11 were a snowstorm of citizen reports.

But Leo said that our mutual Russian friend Sergei also knew who this person was, and had vouched for him. That made me feel a little more grounded in reality. Even though I'd met Sergei only a few weeks earlier, I'd experienced a connection with him that felt as if it would last. It was a prototypical case of trust at first sight.

But trust at first sight is uncommon, and it's not nearly as effective for sizing people up as their belief that they'll know you for a long time.

When somebody thinks they'll have a long relationship with you, they'll usually treat you well, because they know they'll eventually face consequences—good or bad—some of which may last for years.

That's just one of those laws of human nature that make many of the tenets of the social sciences almost as viable and predictable as those of the physical sciences.

So I jotted notes while Leo talked, and took them to my Jedi Master, Jesse Thorne, the senior agent who'd helped me get to know Leo. Jesse taught me something new almost every day, and this day looked like it would be another.

I read him my notes, ending with the remark about mortality. "What does that mean, 'We are all mortal'? Is it a threat?"

"Not directly. It's a reference to an old JFK speech," he said, "about being close to nuclear war. So I'd say go meet the guy. Save the planet. If you're not busy."

I didn't feel remotely ready to work that kind of case. "How about *you* meet the guy?" I said.

"He doesn't know me."

"Me, either."

"He knows *of* you. Through your friends at the club. He trusts them and they trust you, so he trusts you to trust him." I sifted through the pronouns and got the idea. He was talking about *primacy*. That's an FBI "term of art"—phrases that have specialized meanings within specific professions. He was referring to a "transfer of trust" from one stranger to another through a mutual friend.

"But this isn't a 9/11 lead," I said, "so I can't work it. Even if I wanted to." I started to pace.

"Robin, take a breath! Don't sweat this."

"How can you *not* sweat this?"

"Agents don't sweat," Jesse said. "They think."

The second he said that, I knew I'd always remember it. It was some of the best advice I've ever gotten, because type-A people like me are notorious worriers, who are often vulnerable to emotional hijacking. We're classic best enemies: ambitious to a fault.

Even after this incident, though, it took me years to stay rational, stick to my systems, and do the legwork. Work is never easy, but I'd take it over worry any day.

"Let's go to the garage and see a friend of mine." He meant the garage of the FBI building, which was for many months the makeshift headquarters for all the bosses.

On the way over, Jesse said that a program director he knew—an Assistant Special Agent in Charge—was great at tweaking the bureaucracy and making things happen. "He's not a *career* guy," Jesse said. That was one of his highest compliments. He cared about people, not pedigrees, and thought his own success came directly from his dependable, predictable relationships—even more than from his case outcomes, long hours, or awards. So he put great effort into his ultimate goal of finding the specific people he could count on and who relied on him. The resulting relationships had been portable, moving from case to case, office to office, and into the personal realm. Business done right is always personal.

We found Jesse's friend sitting at a picnic table in the garage that served as his command post, and told him the story. "To go ahead with this," the supervisor said, "a source needs to call the tip line—and they can assign somebody even if it's not a 9/11 case."

That wasn't going to happen. Leo's contact clearly wanted anonymity.

Before I could say anything, Jesse pulled out his phone and looked quizzically at his friend, who shrugged and nodded. They shared the shorthand of nonverbal communication.

The supervisor, Jack Johnson, was kind of a cowboy. He did his own thing in his own time.

Jesse dialed the tip line and handed me his new phone, which looked like a walkie-talkie. We were in awe of it. A phone rang at an agent's desk a few feet away, and I reported the tip while we looked at each other. "Can you assign it to Robin Dreeke, please?"

The guy looked at Jesse's buddy, who nodded his head. Then he said, "You got it," and hung up.

"There's one condition," Jack said. "I don't know you, Robin, so I need Jesse on this in a support mode."

"Robin doesn't need me," Jesse said, "but I'd be happy to help." Jack suddenly seemed to look at me through new eyes. From that point on, he became one of my allies. I learned that trust can be transferred at warp speed.

Some veteran agents, though, would have freaked out over working for a relative newbie, but not Jesse. He never got emotionally hijacked, and had almost a psychic ability to read people. He thought *anybody* could. I can't. Never could. That's why I was building my system.

While we were headed to meet the new CHS, I asked Jesse what our immediate agenda was.

"Make friends," he said. "Real fast. But honor his tempo. If we push too hard or fast, he'll walk. Always make it about him. And don't fall *in like* with him. We don't have time to sort that out."

We arrived at a quiet SoHo restaurant where our man was already sipping some kind of tea I'd never heard of. Good sign: Punctuality expresses respect, and anything that reveals somebody's personal tastes—even if it's just tea—indicates openness. On another level: *Agents* are supposed to arrive first, to assert control over the interview.

But the man—named Annan, as in "anonymous"—was so outgoing and charming that he allowed us to guide the conversation.

The short version: Annan was, according to him, very close to the power-elite of one of the world's few nations armed with nuclear weapons. (That's as close as I can get to full disclosure.) His country, he said, was eyeball-to-eyeball with another nuclear nation over old wounds that had recently been reopened. The possible conflagration—largely off the U.S. radar due to our preoccupation with 9/11—was building to a flash point.

All we really knew was that both countries had many unknown factors influencing them, and were ruled by people we did not trust. Now the two nations were locked into the nuclear nightmare scenario that has haunted the globe since World War II.

Jesse's look told me he thought Annan was full-bore serious. It was one of those looks that you try to forget but can't.

The timing could not have been worse, but that was probably all part of somebody's plan. The world's most powerful governments were already in a state of crisis, approaching panic, and this conflict appeared to be a potential tipping point that could trigger a bloodbath: regionally, and possibly internationally.

Both countries were vocally antagonistic to America, and we could easily become a secondary target. But Annan wanted America to step into the middle of this dangerous situation and broker a less incendiary standoff.

Jesse suggested we introduce the information into a very high-level process called the Raw Intelligence Cycle, to get it in front of the country's primary decision makers, free from any mention in the news.

Annan reiterated that he was afraid of dealing with people who had vast political agendas, which were often partly professional and partly personal.

He said he had a contact "at the mountaintop," as he put it, of his country's government, and he believed the best way to defuse the situation was to include only a few people at the highest, most secretive level of foreign relations. He didn't trust the depersonalized machines of power that run virtually all governments.

As he spoke, he seemed distracted, as if he was worried about being seen with us. It's an absolutely common concern of any new CHS. Jesse made a direct comment about Annan's unease, which was how he always worked: everything on the table—no secrets and no surprises.

Annan thanked him for noticing. What he was doing, Annan said, could trigger the wrath of several different sources, who were all diametrically opposed to the others, and not known for respecting human rights. His country had a long tradition of political assassinations, so we saw the full scope of his risk, and understood the depth of his courage.

Annan and I had some things in common. We were both former

naval officers—though I'd gone marines—had kids the same age, loved fishing, and were dedicated dads and husbands. We'd read many of the same books and considered ourselves Stoics. He was even familiar with the Epictetus quote, "It's not what happens to you, but how you react to it that matters."

But I wasn't sure I trusted him, or that he trusted me. Because what did I *really* know about him? What did *he* know about me?

Neither of us, it seemed, had time to find out. As a rule, intelligence operations happen in slow motion, because they're almost always built on trust—and trust can take years to generate, even when trust-building is your day job.

When we got back to the car, I felt more overwhelmed than ever.

Jesse just looked interested—happy to be doing something important—and somewhat amused, mostly by me, I have to admit. "Don't start worrying again," Jesse said. "I just need to mull this thing over a little. It would be good if you could get more data points about him, and the situation in general. But we'll need it in a day or two."

"How can I do *that*?"

He shrugged. "By hurrying."

"Okay."

"But stay focused. Eliminate distractions. Work efficiently."

"Okay."

I still remember every detail, because it was scary. What if this guy was just manipulating us toward a disaster? His avowed country had been hostile toward us most of my life. What if he was al-Qaeda and had come at me by tricking Leo? What if he was just nuts?

Over the next few days, I was never more aware that I needed some kind of fast-forward mechanism to size people up. Jesse did it naturally—but I wasn't Jesse.

If I'd had time—like a month or so—I thought I'd be able to figure this guy out. If I'd known him for a year, I wouldn't even be sweating. But I didn't have a month, or even a week. Time was not on my side. That was the deep, dark hole that I was looking down.

The Theory of Relativity

As I've mentioned, one of the best ways to compile the data points on people is simply to know them for a long time—and to make them feel as if they will *continue to know you,* which makes them feel accountable for all their actions.

But the monkey wrench with that element of behavioral analysis is—guess what? *It takes a long time.* But the effects of time can be altered, with the right hacks.

One extremely helpful work-around is to recognize the fact that time is extremely relative—especially from a behavioral standpoint—as demonstrated by a popular quote from Albert Einstein: "When you sit with a pretty girl for two hours, you think it's only a minute, but when you sit on a hot stove for a minute, you think it's two hours. That's relativity."

So a remarkably effective way to size people up is to perceive the best in them and show them the same attractive qualities in yourself. If you do, time with them will fly—from the perception of both parties—and your insight into them will quickly deepen into a healthy, predictable relationship.

But if people are resistant, it's easy to get stuck in the strict confines of linear time. When that happens, it can be hard to find people who think that they will be in a relationship with you for a long time.

This has become especially true lately, since technology has created an increasingly myopic, moment-driven, and mobile society.

When you do find people who believe they'll have a long relationship with you, though, you can reasonably predict that they'll be more honest, generous, and cordial—and much more willing to support your goals, which they will probably perceive as being *linked with their own.* So once again we see that the signs of trust are complementary and synergistic.

It's better when someone realizes on their *own* that they expect to be in a long relationship with you, but it holds similar power if you initiate that belief. The belief is potent even if you're linked by a completely arbitrary situation, such as being college roommates, next-door neighbors, or the two newest people in a small company. No matter how the coupling occurs, it carries similar consequences and opportunities.

But remember the Einstein Relativity Rule: If you consciously put yourself in the right situation, you can accelerate the process, and transcend time.

My behavioral analysis colleague Jack Schafer has identified three elements that can change the perception of time: duration, intensity, and proximity. In effect, they *accelerate the tempo.* He also taught me a few tricks for *accelerating* the perception of time. Here are the main tricks I've learned over the years.

FIVE HACKS TO ACCELERATE THE TEMPO OF A RELATIONSHIP

1. Intensify the experience. You've probably noticed that when you pack a lot of experiences into one day, the day seems longer. Simple geographic changes, such as flying cross-country, can also make the hours expand, even when time zones don't change. To make a recent relationship feel longer, saturate the time with intense experiences. This happens with soldiers in battle, and anyone who undergoes a traumatic event with you. It also happens in happy experiences, such as falling in love, vacationing together, going to a movie, or buying somebody lunch when they get a promotion.

Take people out of their routines, off autopilot, and outside their zones of defense.

2. Ritualize the relationship. Rituals memorialize moments, mark the passage of time, and have the power to expand time.

Bring someone their favorite coffee drink every Friday, or send a note on any kind of anniversary. Even just reminiscing works.

3. Begin at the end. You do this by trusting people soon after you've met. It pushes time, and isn't as risky as it sounds if you stay reasonable. Remember: *Doveryai no Proveryai*—Trust, but verify. (Which is even easier to remember in Russian, because it rhymes.)

Almost everybody can be trusted to do something, even if it's just to stay out of your way. If they can't, but you're still friendly, they'll be okay.

4. Demonstrate people's value. It heightens their feeling of affiliation with you and promotes their honesty and generosity. People feel like they can be themselves around you. Every moment of your life when you have the pleasure of acting *exactly the way you feel* can stretch linear time majestically.

In friendships, people often experience this time-stopping freedom. If you can bring those golden moments to a professional relationship, people will bring their best selves to you.

5. Decode the "Code of Trust." In my last book, I created a system called the Code of Trust, a five-point formula for *inspiring people to trust you*.

The Code of Trust parallels the Six Signs for Behavior Prediction because you usually *can't trust people who don't trust you*.

So one of the best ways to find people that you can trust is to reverse engineer the Code of Trust and look at yourself from *their perspective*. I call this reverse engineering process "decoding trust."

When you apply the five principles of the Code of Trust to *yourself*—from the perspective of someone you are sizing up—and if you think that they don't find you trustworthy, try to show them that you really do follow these five basic principles:

1. Suspend your ego. If other people think you're an egomaniac, they'll be put off and you won't see the best side of them. They'll be wary, offended, defensive, and often unfriendly. They won't trust you to be fair—and you'll feel the same. To fix the situation, let *them* be the center of attention, and you'll begin to see the best in them.

2. Validate people. If people don't think you approve of them, they'll pull away and look for people who do. We're all like that. But if you keep an open mind—and talk to them about their likes, dislikes, experiences, abilities, and problems—they'll feel comfortable around you, and will be themselves. When that happens, you usually like what you see, because most people do have common decency—and common decency is the common ground of humankind.

3. Don't judge people. If you do, they'll judge you back, even if that's something they don't usually do. When they start judging you, you'll stop seeing their kindness, intelligence, and fairness. You'll just pull away, and that will be the end of it.

4. Be reasonable. If you're reasonable with people, they'll probably be reasonable with you. When you are rational and fair, they'll generally mirror that perception, and you'll have good reason to trust and admire them.

5. Be generous. If you're not, people will be tempted to be selfish around you, just to even things out. Nobody wants to be in a one-sided relationship. Try to give people a little *more* than they expect. If you go the extra mile for people, that mile will be the one they'll remember. When they do, they'll be grateful, and want to return the kind and wise behavior.

When people see that you are following this code of common decency and common sense, most of them will give you the best of themselves.

Another way to use the Code of Trust is to simply start looking for those five traits in other people. They're pretty easy to spot, and the people who follow this code carefully are usually quite predictable and consistent. They're transparent, they want to know what you think, and they talk in terms of your priorities instead of theirs. They acknowledge that your opinions are understandable—even when they don't share them—and they refuse to be emotionally hijacked every time someone goes off the deep end and engages in emotional game playing.

I have taught this code to thousands of FBI agents, and thousands of people in the private sector.

FBI agents tend to pick up the code quickly, because it is so valuable during investigations. So do the master salespeople in the companies that I've made presentations to, because they've virtually all been doing it intuitively for the entirety of their careers. As a rule, the same is *not* true of people who *fail* at salesmanship. Similarly, the FBI agents who struggle most with this code are usually those whose primary concern is their own career.

When you treat someone in a way that's consistent with the code, they usually tell you the truth—even after they've hidden it from other people, who often just make them feel defensive.

Some people think it's ironic that generous, humble, reasonable, nonjudgmental people are quite often more successful than people who are egocentric, self-serving, and full of blame. I don't. Even though we live in a world where treacherous people amass power and money, these are also the people who so often fall from grace, become their own worst enemies, lose the few friends they've got, and don't even enjoy the process.

By now, you probably recognize the contrasts between trustworthy, reliable people and those who aren't.

It's easy for me to size people up now, but only because I created a system for it, rooted in the tells of trust. Now I'll make it easier for you, with more details on how to decode the tells.

A Deeper Dive into the Tells of Trust

As I mentioned in previous chapters, the tells of trust must always be accepted simply as data: objective, tangible, observable behaviors—often occurring repeatedly—that can be reasonably expected to continue.

The tells are not intended to reveal moral character, nor likability. They reveal only *predictability*.

As such, they are the best indicators of the *six main signs for behavior prediction*.

Here's more granularity on how to identify the four ways that the tells of trust and distrust are conveyed:

SPOT THE TELLS

1. Through people's actions.

- Actions are the single most accurate component of the tells, because they speak louder than words and make things happen.
- Current or very recent actions create the best tells of all, but past actions over a long period of time count, too. But these have to be corroborated by objective, observable, verifiable records or references, including public and private sources of information.
- Among the most important current actions are someone's reactions to *your* actions, because they occur in real time, in the real world, and within a context that both parties understand. Actions need to be consistent with stated goals and intentions. *Any conflict* is a terrible tell.

2. Through verbal communication.

- Most people are quite willing to honestly state their beliefs and positions, because it's their best way to get what they want. People love sharing their thoughts with a non-judgmental person. The content of the verbal communication must be rational, relevant, factual, and nonjudgmental. Any major statement that appears to deviate from this can't be fully trusted.

- The style of delivery should be simple, clear, polite, and free from manipulative tricks, such as debating tactics or irrational appeals to emotion. Good communicators must also be good at active listening, and offer immediate, direct answers and questions of their own. You can *never* ask too many questions.

3. Through nonverbal communication.

- **Body language** must be absolutely consistent with someone's verbal message. If the two don't match, it creates the creepy communication style referred to as that of a manipulative used-car salesman.

  When you spot any significant discrepancies between verbal and nonverbal communication, be on the lookout for *false promises, lies, hidden truths, exaggeration, and insincerity.* Any one of them can totally derail an otherwise effective presentation.

- **Facial expressions** are the most revealing form of body language, and the easiest to interpret. Among the most common expressions that reveal stress are: a forced smile, poor eye contact, a furrowed forehead, compressed eyebrows, and compressed lips. Positive facial expressions that help *confirm comfort* with you include eye contact that is frequent but not constant; a slight tilting of the head; a moderate narrowing of the eyes when listening; occasional elevation of the eyebrows; and natural, unforced smiling.

- **Full-body nonverbals** that reveal a disconnect between what someone is saying and how they really feel include the stress gestures of: folding the arms across the chest;

clenching the teeth; keeping the palms down or out of sight; a posture that is notably rigid or slumped; a body position that is slightly turning away and back, or even angled toward an exit.

Comfort is reinforced by open, relaxed actions, including: standing or sitting at a slight angle; moving calmly and smoothly; nodding the head occasionally to show attention and agreement; leaning forward while listening; and open displays, such as palms facing upward while speaking, centered around the abdominal area. Some experts in nonverbal communication advise people to subtly match the other person's movements, but if someone notices that you're doing this, it backfires.

4. Through people's stated and observed intentions.

- Intent that is only implied or assumed is notably unreliable. To believe someone's intent, you need to see clear signs of it, or at least hear a logical, articulate statement of it.
- The most revealing element of someone's stated intent is their description of their short-term, long-term, and ultimate goals. Among these, their short-term goals will have the most immediate impact upon you, but their ultimate goals most accurately reveal their core self, and what they see as their priorities and best interests.
- Their stated intent must clearly reflect their sense of their own best interests. If it doesn't, it probably won't last.

Here are ten of the most common tells that indicate people do *not* think they will have a long relationship with you. They are therefore much harder to size up. When you spot these tells of distrust, be cautious!

Sometimes you'll see them in people you like, who seem also to like you. The affection may be quite genuine, but don't let it fool you. It's not the same as trust, reliability, and competence.

1. Your supervisors often forget your name but don't seem to care. It's another example of the silent language of scorn, which speaks volumes.

Not everyone is good with names, but almost all people seem to miraculously remember the names of people who are important to their future.

Don't buy a house. Rent. Month-to-month.

2. You were hired on a temporary contract, and no effort is being made to extend it. Working temp isn't a great indication to begin with, but if you've been somewhere long enough to make an impression, this is an even worse tell.

Gather your guts and ask—in a rational way—what you can do to be a better resource for your boss and the company. The only qualities of your personality that this direct, proactive response will hurt will be your shyness or lack of self-esteem—but those are qualities you *don't* want.

Watch closely for the general nonverbals of acceptance that I mentioned, which include an overall body position called body blading, in which the person stands slightly sideways, to avoid looking overly aggressive. Other friendly, inviting nonverbals include head tilting, an upbeat expression, and solid eye contact that doesn't petrify into a stare.

If you get a lukewarm response that lacks the clarity and transparency you were hoping for, determine what function or service you can do better than most people, and start doing it. It may be your only ticket to a longer stay.

3. Your supervisors confine virtually all workplace conversations with you to a nonpersonal, surface level. This is common during the early days of employment, but if they don't seem to realize that you're a human being, you're either failing at your job or failing at being a human being.

Act like who you *are*. It's not a dangerous strategy—unless you're a jerk—and will probably break the ice enough to integrate you more fully into your position.

It's easy for bosses to say good-bye to people they don't really know. Make your termination a hard conversation for a boss to have, and it will be less likely to happen.

4. Other employees in similar, related positions tend to hear important information before you do. This means you're not in the prime information loop. Find out why. To survive at a company, you *need situational awareness*. Survival usually has very little to do with charm. It's about getting the job done.

Again, be proactive, because these are difficult days for surviving business bureaucracies. When you don't hear about something that would have allowed you to do your job more productively—and be of benefit to your boss, peers, or others in the company—share your concern with people and seek their advice on how to make the information flow better, in order to enhance *their* success.

Passive people—who don't have information or situational awareness—often disappear into the woodwork and wonder why their careers never take off.

5. Your supervisor never asks you about your long-term career goals. Bad, bad sign. Ultimate language of silence!

Ask them if you can have a conversation in which you share your goals with them. Maybe they thought you were satisfied with staying exactly where you are, and are content to stagnate and remain expendable.

You can start the conversation by asking in a respectful way what *their* goals are. Don't expect people to know more about you than you do about them. Remember: The center of your universe is you, and the center of their universe is them.

6. You aren't included in any work-related social events. It's similar to people forgetting your name, or not talking to you about anything other than work. People are people—but only when they act like it. If they don't, they're just a function—a suit—without an identity.

Focus on someone who seems to like or respect you, and ask them if they want to get a drink or snack after work, or have lunch. It never hurts to tell them the bill's on you. Put some effort into your own positive nonverbals. Find out if the company, office, or group has a social networking page where they share info.

7. A peer employee is rude to you. Try to determine if it's because other people have been talking smack about you. That's easier than you may think, because people are attracted to gossip in the same way they like to look at a wreck. Do not reciprocate. Rise above it.

8. You volunteer to expand your role, but your boss rejects the offer. It happens. If it keeps happening, it means you're a cog in a wheel. One reason may be that you are offering resources in areas that are already covered. Seek to understand their priorities, and ask them what is falling short, and how you can be a resource.

With alarming speed, though, people are dismissed when they're considered replicable.

Start expanding your role on your own—gratis. When people around you get something for nothing, they want it to continue, and sooner or later they'll reward it. Your reward is that there is a "later."

9. You feel as if there are cliques around you that don't welcome your presence. You're probably right—rather than paranoid—because cliques by definition are exclusive.

To become a member, perform one of the most difficult but rewarding feats in all of business culture: *Humble yourself.* Humility is incredibly rewarding—it's Trust 101. It's hard to reject humble people—it's like kicking somebody who's down.

10. Supervisors talk to some of your peers about the future, but leave you out. It's probably because they don't see you as part of the future.

To turn that around, *ask* about the future. Show interest. Make it clear that you not only want to be part of it, but want to help others be part of it. That makes *your* intent part of *their* intent.

Because people do what's in their own best interests, if your presence enhances that, you'll be much more likely to stick around.

April 2002
The Second Meeting

The hardest part of my second meeting with Annan was being allowed to attend it. When Jesse and I reported the outcome of the first meeting—a plausible threat of nuclear war—we got bumped up to a much higher, risk-averse supervisor: the type who's just a career-in-a-suit. He was clearly concerned that this hot-potato case could blow up in his face and kill his upward mobility. He vented some of his anxiety by telling me he needed somebody on this who had more experience.

I picked up on Jesse's attitude and didn't let myself get freaked out by the assault on my competence. The most important element in controlling *this case*, I found, was to control *myself.* For the first time on a major case, I just looked at this as an opportunity to manage the system—as Jesse had when he'd let me call in my own lead—and to strategize my relationships. The shift in my attitude was incredibly liberating. I felt like I had a new superpower: *thinking instead of sweating,* and focusing on the people as much as the process.

I still wanted to control the situation, but sometimes the best way to control things is to let go, and just do what you can to shift things in your direction—which is usually to be a resource for them, helping them to go in *their* own direction. It's definitely a Zen concept, but there's a reason why Dale Carnegie's famous book isn't called *How to Win Friends and Control People*.

As I talked to the new supervisor, I started to look at the situation from his perspective, and made it clear, with facts and figures, that I understood his concerns. Some of the points I made were even critical of my inclusion. But why not? Genuine, self-critical honesty is a great way to help people respect and admire you. It's the ultimate in transparency, and when you're transparent about your own shortcomings or question your own strategies, *other people don't have to*—which often results in them making your case *for* you. It's scary the first few times you do it, but it works wonders.

This strategy changed his attitude toward me. He was still vetting me for competence, but he started to look for reasons to keep me on the case instead of kicking me off it.

Then I threw myself into what felt like an endless day and night of research on every little detail Annan had offered, double-checking against information from other national security agencies. Every bit of Annan's information—his ground truth—checked out perfectly.

I got the go-ahead to stay on the case.

To get ready for the meeting—a process that agents call "crafting the encounter"—I rented a room at a nice hotel, ordered tea service from the front desk, and found the one store in Manhattan that had Annan's favorite tea. I was trying to intensify the tempo of cooperation by ritualizing our relationship, and taking liking to the next level.

I didn't need to worry about intensifying the *experience*. The people who had their fingers on the nuclear button were taking care of that.

The tea I bought, though, was not the right tone of pink—so I put a drop of food coloring in it, then waited for Annan to call from the lobby. When he did, I poured a glass of the pink tea into a teacup that was reminiscent of his country. And then spilled the whole damn thing down my leg. The food coloring wouldn't come out. The best-case scenario was that Annan would think I'd wet my pants.

But he didn't. I think he saw through my innocent chicanery and was actually flattered by it. That was probably part of his own natural desire to intensify the tempo: by being reasonable, and by beginning at the end, with his own leap of trust.

Outcome: excellent! He opened up further, and shared the fact that he was a very close relative of the president of his country. That was extremely encouraging for Jesse and me, because it meant we wouldn't have to crawl through the usual gauntlet of yes-men, whose primary job is to say no.

For Annan, though, those ultraclose ties were a mixed blessing, because his country, as I mentioned, had a penchant for solving problems with high-level assassinations. If the operation he was proposing went south, his relative might be deposed and imprisoned, and Annan and his family, all in America at the moment, might never enjoy another safe day for the rest of their lives.

The biggest prize of the meeting, though, was learning that Annan's relative was belligerent to the United States mostly just for the *sake of show*—to appease the other nations in his part of the world, almost all of which were openly hostile to us. His own country also had many radical, anti-American factions, and ignoring them—with their ability and willingness to launch suicide missions—could be deadly.

We gave Annan several statements to pass to his relative. If the leader was willing to say them publicly, in situations that would be reported by international news outlets, we would know that Annan's claims and assessments were bona fide.

By the end of the week, each of the statements was in the news. America stepped into the conflict to craft a nonviolent accord. Annan's relative was vitriolic—absolutely venomous about America—as Annan had said he would be. And he complied perfectly. He ordered his army to stand down. Then withdraw. The other country "won" the standoff.

Peace was achieved. The incident became a small part of the history of the post-9/11 world. The full truth was never revealed.

It was the beginning of my very long, very close friendship with Annan.

Over time, Annan and I exercised virtually all of the tenets that signify the belief in—and power of—a long relationship.

Most of these tells are very common in the workplace, and are usually between employees and their immediate supervisors, but they are also peer to peer.

In the final analysis, *trust is trust*—whether among people or vast groups of nations—and the most fundamental principles of trust are universal.

The following tells are portable and widely applicable, because each one is a direct reflection of the one force that animates all valid theories in the science of behavioral analysis: human nature.

TEN POSITIVE TELLS FOR THE PERCEPTION OF
LONGEVITY IN A RELATIONSHIP

1. People regularly invite you to participate in their own long-term goals. It's a significant signal that they not only want you around for a long time, but also trust you with their future.

This indicates two signs at once—vesting, and the perception of a long relationship—wrapped in a sweet package of positive action.

It's very close to a partnership, although not always an equal partnership. It doesn't matter: Time is the more important tell.

2. People consistently choose to establish and expand traditions centered on your relationship with them. The traditions can consist of virtually anything—from a favorite restaurant to a favored bourbon—but the premise or setting should reflect the nature of your bond with them.

These special moments can be the perfect time to express your feelings about their importance in your life.

These events reflect not just positive action, but also positive emotion—often expressed with nonverbal communication, including strong eye contact, animated facial expressions, and a sense of energy.

3. People are almost always enthusiastic about including you in their sphere of influence. This is a golden tell, because it shows you—and others—that you are a member of an inner circle, even if it's a large circle that includes people with various levels of intimacy and power.

A genuine display of enthusiasm is vitally important, because it reflects not just positive action, but also positive emotion, typically driven by dopamine and other feel-good neurotransmitters. Once again, these emotions are often expressed with nonverbal communication, including strong eye contact, animated facial expressions, and a sense of energy.

4. People see you as hard to replace. Celebrate: Many people do everything they can to be irreplaceable and still don't achieve it.

That's frequently because they're in a position that can be filled by another highly skilled person, but sometimes it's because their supervisors, for reasons of their own, don't really want them to achieve the reward of longevity.

If you continually excel and sacrifice without reward, you're working for someone you should not trust, even if they're pleasant and charming. But if your supervisor acknowledges your special value and finds ways to enhance it, you can probably trust them to act in your own best interests.

5. People periodically give you promotions, commendations, or recognition. Even if the perks or upgrades are relatively minor, they tell you that you've been noticed and validated. That's usually a strong sign of enhanced job security for the foreseeable future. It also indicates that if you do make a significant mistake, you probably won't lose your job.

The recognition is a message to other people that you're doing well, which usually prompts widening respect, consideration, and cooperation.

All of this goodwill reinforces your longevity, and your longevity enhances the goodwill.

6. People give you perks and benefits that are consistent with a long-term relationship. This can include the ability to shift your hours as needed, because they trust you to get the job done. It could also include your own choices on office decor, a generous vacation schedule, or upper-tier benefits. Even if you don't have a high salary, these tells still indicate that your bosses plan on having you around for an extended period.

The people you work for are expressing their desire to keep you there with the one thing that's more powerful than words: action.

Sometimes this happens when you're hired, which is an excellent signal of security, and sometimes it's a reward for achievement, which is even better.

Either way, it allows you to relax about impressing people, which can allow you to indulge in the extremely valuable trait of creativity, a quality that's usually inhibited by insecurity.

7. People encourage you to attend seminars, conferences, trainings, or college classes. This is especially telling if they include the work as part of your employment or if they pay for some or all of the expenses.

This is rarely extended to people who aren't expected to achieve longevity. When people with power actively participate in increasing your skills and knowledge, it not only signifies your security, but makes you more valuable to them—and also more valuable to their competitors, which helps shift the power differential in your direction.

Don't hesitate to send a thank-you note. (Your mother was right about good manners.)

8. People include you in work-related social activities. This shows that they value you as a whole person and want other associates to get to know you. Both of those factors influence longevity.

When someone thinks of you as a person rather than as a cog in a wheel, they're more patient about problems. When they know that other people in the organization consider you a friend, they're even more respectful.

This tell is especially important if some of the activities consist mostly of people who are above you in the professional hierarchy. This elevates you from being a standard employee to being "one of the family." In relatively small workplaces, this tell is relatively common and is practically a requirement for long-term relationships and employment.

9. People usually say "we" instead of "you" or "I." When this happens during discussions of long-term goals or the future of the organization, it's pure essence of verbal bonding!

Some people use pronouns that imply inclusion just to be polite, so it's important to note who else they address that way and what else they say to indicate you are a part of their future.

Another clue is when someone gradually switches from "I" to "we" over an extended period, during which your relationship with them has deepened and withstood the test of time.

Like so many other elements that create trust, it can help if you lead the way in saying "we." As always, one of the surest ways to find a trustworthy person is to trust them.

10. People never seem to take you for granted. The dark side of longevity is that when you work so well for so long, people assume that what you do is easy.

This is so painfully common that we're all guilty of it from time to time, but rarely because of arrogance or lack of appreciation. It's a law of human nature that no one can fully understand us other than ourselves—and sometimes even *we* fail at that.

Even so, we suffer alone but we survive together.

So if you find someone who acts as if each of your achievements has succeeded beyond all expectations, you can trust them with your future.

Most of these tells—or equivalents of them—emerged in my last physical contact with Annan, in 2018. As in the previous chapter, I'll help you spot them by noting the numbers that I assigned to each one.

January 2018
Final Moments

Annan ultimately became my longest-tenured CHS, and one of my best and oldest friends. Some business cultures are ambivalent about emotional ties among coworkers, fearing they might cloud judgment and blur hierarchies, but I know of few things more satisfying than blending two of the most powerful forces in human life: friendship and work.

It allows a dual experience of intimacy rivaled only by that of family, which also combines the element of survival with the equally primal impulse of love.

Success for both types of interactions requires a healthy, meaningful relationship. The cross-over nature of the relationship doesn't allow much of a margin for error.

So in 2018, when Annan called me and said he was in desperate need of help, I immediately told him I would do everything I could—even before he told me what the problem was. I think that's appropriate among those closest to you, because it elevates your response to the highest level of personal and professional regard. If it turns out to be something you just can't do—which is rare, because people close to you already know what you can and can't do—the person will almost always understand.

"A friend of mine," Annan said, "is being misrepresented in the press in regard to a mass shooting." Like anyone else who had watched the news that day, I'd heard about it. It was horrific.

"I must ask you to help stop that," Annan said. "But if you can't, I'll understand" (Positive Tell #10).

"I will. Absolutely. Right now." I planned to verify Annan's belief—*Doveryai no Proveryai*—but I was almost certain, after a seventeen-year relationship, that his request was legitimate.

He said that his friend was the father of a young man who had just committed one of the worst shootings in U.S. history, but the FBI was also investigating the father, Annan's friend, because the shooter had used his father's computer to contact religious extremists. The media had discovered this investigation, and the father, who was already torn to pieces by the tragedy, was now the source of speculation that threatened to haunt him forever—even after he'd been proven innocent.

"Meet me in two hours," I told Annan.

I didn't need to tell him where, because he and I had been meeting for many years at the same restaurant, which reflected his ethnicity. We even ordered the same pink tea we'd drunk in 2002, as the only existing memorial of a peace accord that might not have been, if Annan hadn't been so brave at that dreadful time (Positive Tell #2).

I immediately called a close FBI colleague who worked in the field office that was covering the case, and I shared my information with him, trusting that he'd do a solid job, because of our past relationship (Positive Tell #5). He said he'd drop everything and get on it right away (Positive Tell #6).

My associate's help, and my input—combined with the existing investigation—almost immediately shifted the focus on the father: from being a possible suspect to being a helpful resource on the case.

I waited for Annan outside the restaurant—in a private place, because I knew the good news would trigger his emotions.

It did. He embraced me, unable, at that moment, to say anything.

I gave him a moment alone to call his friend. We entered the restaurant with great relief, floating on our camaraderie.

Annan—who was preparing to move back to his homeland, which was much safer now—presented me with a framed photo of us back in the old days (Positive Tell #6). We both stared at it for a long moment, silently, each probably thinking different thoughts, but feeling exactly the same way.

Now came the hard part. Annan had previously asked me to invest in a company he was starting, but at this time I had to decline. His offer was generous (Positive Tell #5), but there were federal ethics issues that made it impossible for me to invest. He mentioned, though, that because I would soon be retiring from the FBI, he would keep the offer wide open, and that "we can do it then" (Positive Tell #9).

I knew he was sincere, so I had to tell him that I was afraid his business might not work. I feared that his natural optimism—which was an important part of his courage—would get the best of him (and it did, causing him to lose his new home).

He was very casual when I declined the offer, but I knew he was disappointed. I looked into his eyes, reached out my hand, and said, "I'm sorry." That was enough—more than enough—between old friends.

We both knew that this business was simply a different situation from the ones that had bonded us, and we both had learned over the years that trust and affiliation must always be offered *in their full context:* the intersection of a person plus the situation.

They've both got to be right. That's one of the toughest demands of maintaining a personal relationship in a business situation, since business situations change far more often than people do.

It was sad to see him go. I would miss working with him, even though my role was now changing. Even after retirement, I knew I would still do a good deal of work on behalf of national security, sometimes with old contacts, and at some point it might include him.

But when that happened I would pass the work on to others and let *them* make the critical decisions. It would be different. The most constant element of life is change. It can't be avoided.

But it can be mourned, or at least memorialized.

At the point of our parting, we both knew that many of our memories of shared difficulties—sometimes requiring great courage in moments of historic upheaval—would eventually fade to moments of almost-forgotten glory, never to come again.

"Are you coming to my retirement party?" I asked him.

"Of course! It's mine, too" (Positive Tell #4).

"It will be good to see your family. It's been weeks."

Now that the stress of his wrongly suspected friend had subsided, a new reality was weighing upon us: We would soon be continents apart—as would our wives and kids, all bonded now.

"Thank you for what you did today," he said as we prepared to leave, both with obligations still to be met, none of which would be remembered.

"Thank you for these years of service. To my country," I said.

"To *our* country. And to *you*," he said.

I watched him walk away.

Agents don't sweat. But they certainly do tear up from time to time.

DEBRIEFING

CHAPTER 4:
"MAKE TIME COUNT"

SIGN #2: LONGEVITY

Key Quote: "When somebody thinks they'll have a long relationship with you, they'll usually treat you well, because they know they'll eventually face consequences—good or bad—some of which may last for years."

Key Message: Predicting people accurately is often as dependent upon present-day circumstances as it is on their character, past actions, or intent. A vital sign of those circumstances is their perception of how long they will have close and frequent interactions with you.

THE TAKEAWAYS

1. **Time:** The most problematic element of finding people who think they will be with you a long time is that it *usually takes a long time.* But that perception can be altered with various behavioral techniques.
2. **Primacy:** This is an FBI term for creating the difficult quality of "instant trust." This can be created by transferring the expectation of positive behaviors from one person to another through a mutual acquaintance. It's also called a "transfer of trust."
3. **Lead by example:** It is often possible to predict that people will behave honorably and kindly if you do it first. It can speed the process greatly, by enhancing the perception of duration. The wise, cautious approach is to offer people things of emotional and practical value, such as confidentiality or nonmaterial resources for their priorities.

The Code of Trust: A System for Inspiring Trust in Others

1. **Suspend your ego.** It's not all about you. Ever. The more you think it is, the less it will be true.
2. **Validate people.** Find out who they are and why they do what they do. They'll open up, and you'll find things you like about them.
3. **Don't judge.** It doesn't mean you approve. It means you understand. People want understanding even more than approval.
4. **Be reasonable.** Stick tightly to reality and realism. You'll never get anywhere if you're not real.

5. Be generous. When you go win-win in everything you do, you always win.

Ten Positive Tells for the Perception of Longevity in a Relationship

1. They ask you to participate in their long-term goals.
2. They pay attention to traditions that acknowledge you.
3. They're enthusiastic about including you.
4. They position you as someone who'd be hard to replace.
5. They periodically offer rewards, including promotions.
6. They give you perks that signify a long-term relationship.
7. They encourage you to expand your training.
8. They welcome you to be part of social activities.
9. They typically say "we" instead of "I" or "you."
10. They never seem to take you for granted.

Ten Negative Tells for the Perception of Longevity in a Relationship

1. They forget your name but don't seem to care.
2. They don't mention renewing your temporary contract.
3. They don't try to connect with you on a personal level.
4. You're the last to know about certain important issues.
5. They don't ask about your long-term goals.
6. You aren't included in work-related social events.
7. A peer employee is rude to you.
8. Your offer to expand your role is rejected.
9. It seems as if there are cliques that don't welcome your presence.
10. When people talk about the future, they never mention you.

5

KNOW WHO TO GO TO

Sign #3: RELIABILITY

*Can this person do what they
say they will? And will they?*

**August 2018
Southeastern United States**

America was in the dawning days of threat from a new weapon of mass destruction, and a task force I'd joined was among the first in the FBI to confront it.

As our team leader called the initial meeting to order, I pulled out my tablet to take notes, hungry for what he knew about this developing danger. He had a reputation for brilliance, and he seemed cordial and receptive, so I had no glaring reason not to trust him with this difficult assignment. Besides, his supervisors obviously relied on him, so I assumed I could, too, in a rational and objective transfer of trust.

My readiness to trust the guy—whom I'll call George—was also bolstered by the apparent presence of three of the Six Signs for Behavior Prediction. His past patterns of competence and diligence were stellar (Sign #3: Reliability), and he was known for caring about the success of the people with whom he worked (Sign #1: Vesting). Also, because of the severity of this situation, it looked as if he and I would be linked for a long time (Sign #2: Longevity).

So I had enough secondhand data points on George to make me like and respect him, but not enough yet to make me fully trust him with this part of the national security of the United States. A person at the helm of a project like this needed to be absolutely *reliable:* a quality, as I've mentioned, that consists primarily of *competence* and *diligence.*

Despite my residue of doubt about George, I felt optimistic and receptive—an attitude that has sparked most of the best relationships in my life. Many people, of course, start at the other end of the spectrum of trust, but if you're pessimistic and wary, people usually sense it, react to it, and return it—as golden opportunities die on the vine. Even feeling neutral about someone can, so to speak, leave you stuck in neutral.

The task force was composed of people from several offices, so we started by introducing ourselves in five-minute snippets, talking mostly about the training that had brought us here. When George's turn came, he rose with a look of quiet confidence and squared off into the rectilinear body language of a powerful man facing a momentous challenge. His first words, reflecting the mission statement he'd crafted, grabbed the attention of everybody at the table.

"We're facing a mass destruction weapon of the future," he intoned, "and our mission is to understand it, confine it, control it, and eliminate it. If we do, history may remember this moment. If we don't, God help us all."

We all sat a little straighter, and George seemed to like the effect his words had on us.

Glancing at the three-by-five cards in his hand, he told the story of how he'd been assigned to this position. Then he followed up with a recitation of his greatest hits, so I put down my tablet and waited for him to introduce our agenda of action. But he went off on a tangent about identifying funds, creating processes, and fulfilling the paperwork requirements.

That gave me pause. He'd opened with a galvanizing selling point, but now he was *un*selling it with a sea of digressions that were all delivered with equal verve. Some of the agents were drifting into thousand-yard stares, but I wrote off the jibber-jabber as just a bad case of first-meeting jitters.

I was able to keep my focus, but needed coffee—badly. The problem was, we weren't allowed to put any food or drink on our sleek redwood conference table, which was built along the lines of an aircraft carrier. That's government for you, right? Splurge on a table, and then trust agents enough to stop mass destruction, but not enough to keep their table clean?

I peeked at my watch. *Oh shit.* Forty minutes had passed, and he was still on the story of his life. The day was already dreary with low-hanging clouds, and the shades were drawn—as they are in all of our buildings, all the time—but even so, I couldn't help but marvel at how something as sexy as preventing mass destruction could be reduced to clerical work so dull that it made me rate the day by its weather.

It was a bad tell, because in group situations people don't believe you're competent at something if you can't communicate it. It's part of the package, and I've seen it kill important projects.

As George droned on, it became clear that he was far more adept with technology than with people, which was understandable, since he was in the investigative sector of the FBI, which tends to be tech driven. In my branch—operations—people are the driving force. We find confidential human sources and enlist them in projects, which are, in effect, the products that we brand, market, and sell to supervisors.

George's specialty, which I rarely dealt with, was an area called Flaps and Seals: a surveillance sector that includes covertly opening the envelopes and packages of suspects and foreign threats, using a range of technologies. It's associated with a section known as Locks, Clicks, and Picks, a branch of the Bureau's tradecraft that performs missions requiring clandestine entry into buildings and rooms—black-bag jobs—to find evidence, disable cryptography devices, and deposit surveillance equipment—some of it really cool, like miniature audio-video drones that looked like bugs, called insectothopters. None of this, though, had much to do with people.

But I'll say this for the tech guys: They always had a hell of a lot better toys than we did.

As the clock ticked and my stomach growled, I grew less receptive to George, because he was still stuck in the weeds and was adopting a pontifical tone. Irrelevant information by itself is bad enough, but irrelevant *pontifical* information is unforgivable—and as common as dirt.

I wasn't happy. But so what? If the point of my work was to make me happy, I wouldn't get paid.

Besides, I was at the epicenter of America's response to a game-changing weapon of the future—which was, somewhat ironically, drones. Like many people, I hadn't given much thought to drones as an emerging threat, but one of my field supervisors, Doug Wellborne, had put an end to that.

Doug, who knew that I was a licensed pilot, had called me into his office and told me that the use of drones in criminal and terrorist activities was growing exponentially, and that a task force was being assembled to deal with it, starting with organizing a conference that would include the best minds in the field of unmanned aerial vehicles, or UAVs.

I listened hard to what Doug had to say, because he was a lotto legend: a great boss, totally mission-oriented. He was reliable at whatever he chose to do, because his personality was pure elixir of competence and diligence. When people have as much of both qualities as Doug did, it's almost impossible *not* to rely on them.

Full-bore reliability is a veritable superpower. Reliable, dependable people are so consistently successful at whatever they do that their bosses automatically give them the most important jobs—and look elsewhere when they're searching for weak links, someone to blame, or a victim to downsize.

Like almost all other competent, diligent people, Doug's reliability in the field—free from oversight and scrutiny—invariably tipped the rules of engagement in his favor. He was so accustomed to accomplishment that he believed that virtually everything within the realm of practicality could be achieved, if it was met with enough skill and sweat. Every time I saw him he reminded me of an amazing colonel I had in the marines whose motto was: *Never tell me no. Just tell me what it will cost me.*

Doug was a specialist in weapons of mass destruction, and like other WMD guys in the postmodern, less-is-more era that started after America failed to pacify the Middle East with its vast fighting forces, the specter of drones scared the hell out of him. In the wrong hands, they held the potential to terrorize and control entire populations—with a very limited investment, and terrifying drama.

Drones of up to twenty-seven feet had already been used extensively by the U.S. in the war on terror, and our UAVs had killed an estimated 2,500 people.

But China is the world's largest drone manufacturer, and use of their UAVs was proliferating in the Middle East. ISIS and al-Qaeda didn't have the massive drones that America deploys, but the terrorists were terminally effective with their off-the-shelf models, particularly in swarm formations that were loaded with grenade-sized munitions. These drones were as effective as their handcrafted roadside bombs: the improvised explosive devices called IEDs that had killed and crippled so many soldiers in the Iraq and Afghanistan wars. For the terrorists, drones had become IEDs with wings. Even more distressing, there was growing speculation in the press that ISIS and al-Qaeda were engaged in active measures to unleash UAV strikes on the continental U.S., potentially delivering large payloads of chemical, biological, or radiological material.

In a scenario known as a "balloon drop," a swarm of drones can swoop down on an outdoor stadium—or any crowd—loaded with firearms, hand grenades, or ultratoxic agents, including the deadly poison ricin. Larger drones can be used as vehicles for bombs, including the "dirty bombs" that spread radioactive material.

Drones had also made punk criminals as dangerous as terrorists. Organized crime was not only thriving with the hobby-store models, but also had access to UAVs that cost $30,000 to $50,000. For a cartel, that's chump change. But after the first meeting with George, I could tell that I was going to have to give him a lot of my resources. He was out of his comfort zone and desperately needed a dose of the empowering potion of trust.

I had approximately the same seniority as George and could have requested a shuffle in the leadership of the team—or tried to take it often over myself. But one of the most ironic ingredients of power is that it grows faster when you let go of it, so I had no problem with letting George look like a rock star—if he was up to it.

On the brighter side, I now had a great reason to get a drone pilot's certificate and to spend $1,500 of my own money on a DJI Phantom 4 drone: one that was typical of what some of the bad guys were already using.

I was going to hit the park with my son and get some flying done. In that rush of anticipation—and the satisfaction I get from mastering a new technology—I felt like I'd taken the first step in figuring out George. He was just a hard-core tech guy with a good heart.

The Power of Reliability

In many situations, reliability is virtually synonymous with trust.

You can love someone with all your heart and trust them with your deepest secrets, but there are countless areas in which relying upon that same person would be not just impossible, but insane. You'd never trust an airline pilot to perform your brain surgery, or trust a surgeon to fly your jet. You'll always distrust people in more areas than you trust them.

So be real. You owe it to yourself and to the people you spare from jobs they can't do. And don't overlook the need for both competence *and* diligence.

We all wish that we could rely upon people who are competent but not diligent or diligent but not competent. But we can't, in the real world—and that's the only one we have.

Competence

During the centuries when farming and manufacturing dominated the demands for human survival, reliability was generally so easy to assess that it became a side issue in the American economy. It was simply expected. But in the age of information, managers consistently get fooled—often to disastrous degrees—because the internet provides numerous mechanisms for deceit and manipulation, in matters of information.

Because of this, competence management was recently isolated as a specialty and is now generally addressed by human resource analytics. Unfortunately, though, when new forms of reality checks are devised, people can find ways to subvert them.

That problem places extra importance on knowing the tells of competence and diligence. People will still lie to you, but you'll usually know it when they do.

Bottom line: Expect competence, but dive deep enough to ferret out the phonies. If you find incompetence, make sure it's remedied, or that people are confined to tasks they are capable of completing. If you don't have a competence management team—or even person—find one.

There is also a classic, unchanged factor at play: the so-called "curse of competence." Some people are actually punished for their competence, because less competent coworkers sabotage their success or dump their own work on them.

Competence should be determined before someone is hired, but the conventional hiring process—consisting of a review of résumés, multiple interviews, trial tasks, and reference checks—has long been overrated as an accurate process.

Almost all applicants present their level of competence in the best possible light, and many of them inadvertently overstate it, due to lack of self-awareness, or the belief that they can learn on the job.

Résumés also frequently misrepresent competence, because past employers tend to offer generous assessments, sometimes as a way to soften the blow of dismissing someone, or for their own convenience.

It is also common for highly skilled managers who are involved in the hiring process to overrate candidates, due to the false and overly optimistic assumption that their own level of competence is common, or at least attainable.

The net effect: Competence—a quality that should be easy to determine in a rational, objective way—has become a subjective, irrational popularity contest when assessed only by the conventional and antiquated methods.

Competence isn't just a business problem. In the initial glow of friendship, people often forget that their relationships require a sufficient degree of mutual competence simply to survive in a busy, complex society in which free time exists as a zero-sum factor.

Marriages are even more dependent upon competence than friendships, because they typically include a significant degree of partnership in the practical matters of finances, household work, childcare issues, time management, social activities, legalities and ethics, and goals. Most of the behavioral literature about the causes of marital problems includes as many that are related to competence as to love.

As a rule, if people are competent in their marriages and social relationships, they also tend to be competent professionally. Partly because of this, one of the best tells for competence in both personal and professional relationships is to ask people about multiple areas of their lives—their kids, their spouses, their professions, achievements, and their friendships. This can involve relatively vague "inkblot-test" questions, along the lines of: "Tell me about some of the *personal* challenges you've faced." If people start sharing their thoughts with no overt self-consciousness and with complete transparency, they are far more likely to be honest and accurate about their professional competence.

If they're vague or defensive, they may well be exaggerating their ability to be competent in their work.

When I'm exploring people for tells of competence, I look for *consistency* and *congruence:* consistency of statements when I ask the same question in a couple of different ways, and congruence among all answers, including those that seem to have nothing to do with work.

Even though lack of competence is a dealbreaker in most issues of trust, competence without diligence can be even more insidious, because it can catch you off guard. Being able to do something is not at all the same as actually doing it. So one of the bugs in the equation of reliability is that very competent people often ride the wave of their raw skills, considering diligence to be the sad purview of the worker bees who come in at the end of a project to tie up loose ends and clean up messes.

In that situation, nobody wins, and strife can run rampant. It's the dark side of competence.

Diligence

Human beings are like the *Titanic*: We're very large ships with very small rudders. We all try to steer a straight course, but we typically have more forward motion than sure, steady guidance.

Diligence is one of our primary rudders. It guides us during days of doubt, it course-corrects when we go off track, and it contributes tremendously to the predictability that reliability creates and reflects.

Diligence consists primarily of specific, core qualities of character:

- **Persistence.** There's no easy way to do a hard job.
- **Motivation.** Your work, if your heart is in it, can live long after you die, and travel the world, and with it, a part of your heart.
- **Thoroughness.** If you can't finish, don't start.
- **Attention to detail.** Nobody wants to clean up after you. Not even your mom.

- **An impeccable work ethic.** Work is the great equalizer. It exalts the humble and humbles the exalted.
- **A sense of self-responsibility in all tasks, no matter how minor, or seemingly unrelated.** They call it due diligence because it's *due*—not optional.
- **Consideration for others.** The only measure of love that is true is not how you feel but what you *do*.

Diligence is often even more important than competence, because when diligent people aren't competent at the task you give them, you can generally reassign them to something else. Also, when people are usually competent, but not always—which is very common—their diligence can enable them to achieve full competence.

For the most part, it's easier for diligent people to overcome a lack of competence than it is for competent people to overcome a lack of diligence.

I love working with diligent people, because their problems don't become my problems. They work without drama, don't waste time, don't allow last-minute glitches to occur, don't play office politics, and don't shirk responsibility.

When someone shows diligence, it's important to mention your appreciation for that trait. The relative enthusiasm of their response will help you measure how important that quality is to them. When the work of an extremely diligent person is rewarded, their response will usually be effusive.

The reward doesn't need to be financial, because the primary motivator of character-driven people is sincere, consistent *respect*—even more than money. The best way to reward them is to voice the importance of their value, and seek their thoughts and opinions. Talk to them in terms of their own priorities, validate them nonjudgmentally, empower them with choice, and vest in their goals.

Another way to determine someone's relative diligence is to objectively calculate the *lack* of it in people who are performing poorly. Pollsters say that at least half of all American employees just go through the motions at work. Their lack of diligence shows up in absenteeism, low energy, lack of enthusiasm, and goofing off at work. Many workers who are *not* diligent tend to be quiet and reserved, don't form bonds with coworkers, and work robotically and dispassionately.

Interestingly, most disengaged workers tend to apply the same uninspired mentality to their leisure activities on weekends and after work.

It's estimated that about 50 percent of workers are consistently engaged, 30 percent are only partially engaged, and 20 percent are not at all engaged in their work. Instead of working, many of these people surf the internet, shop online, socialize, play video games, look at social media, take naps, talk on the phone, job hunt, and get snacks and drinks.

That behavior costs American employers approximately 2 percent of our gross domestic product, and companies spend about 20 percent of an unreliable person's salary to replace them.

Many of the companies for whom I consult have told me that they can't recruit an ideal workforce, so they try to make the best of the one they have, in accord with the advice of motivation guru Frank Pacetta, who created the phrase "Don't fire people—fire them up!"

Firing people up starts with figuring them out. Determine their core competencies and do what you can to revive their diligence. One of the most powerful methods for both tasks is to take a leap of trust and vest in their success. Then—*Doveryai no Proveryai!*—give them a task they should be able to do, and see if they do it. Minimize your risks, but let uninspired workers experience the intoxicating atmosphere of a trust-based environment. If they can't make it there, they can't make it anywhere.

That was what I did with George at our second meeting.

George the Second

"Good news!" I told George. "I've got the sharpest guy in the UAV field for our conference."

I described the person I had in mind, who'd come to me through someone I'd known for more than twenty years: a former marine, now CEO of a cryptography lab, who was one of the recruits I had long ago supervised when he was going through the boot camp hell week known as "The Crucible." I'd witnessed the guy's selfless acts of helping fellow recruits, and his diligence, competence, and generosity were still clear in my mind. So I was happy to accept the person he recommended, as a transfer of trust.

"Reach out to him and see if he'll be our keynote speaker," George said.

"Roger that. But I think it would be better if *you* did. You're the leader. You've got the gravitas." That wasn't true yet, but I was trying to make it true.

"On it!" George said. His eyes were bright with the self-respect that arises organically in people when you treat them with trust.

"And ask him about his colleagues," I said, "because he's surrounded by people who work with drones. You could probably fill your whole roster with his people."

"Good find!" he said.

The rest of the second meeting went much better than the first. George started connecting with the task force agents, listening more and talking less. When he did talk, he asked about our thoughts and opinions. I was seeing more flashes of the tells of trust than I had at the first meeting.

Some people would probably think that handing off my contact would undercut my own authority in this important task force, but not me. Leadership is all about sharing power—not consolidating it—and about being a resource for the success of others on your team. People who don't get that are sailing on the same *Titanic* as the people who think the best way to impress others is to tell everybody how great they are.

Much of the rest of the meeting was spent talking about the mechanics of funding and the technicalities of unmanned aerial guidance systems. I was able to follow it much better than before, because I'd attended a series of classes on drones, which was mostly populated by broadcast journalists, who are now using drones extensively.

I was impressed with George's affinity for technology. He had the mind of a scientist, which was probably part of the reason his people skills weren't as strong as his tech skills. I believe that people with extreme gifts in one major area of the intellect, such as math and science, often have corresponding deficits in the areas at the opposite end of the spectrum, which in this case would be language and social skills.

My own proclivity is for the soft sciences of language and social skills—and to be honest, I think that they're actually easier than the hard sciences. That's part of the reason I shifted my major in college from aerospace engineering to political science. But the soft sciences are not less *important*. If anything, to survive and thrive, people skills are probably somewhat more important.

People say that life isn't fair, but it seems pretty fair to me.

The problem is people. *We're* not fair.

TEN NEGATIVE TELLS FOR RELIABILITY (COMPETENCE PLUS DILIGENCE)

1. Unreliable people micromanage without providing real help. Like most of the tells of trust and distrust, this can occur among people below your job status or above it, even though that's not always apparent.

Micromanaging is usually thought of as a problem among managers, but the people they manage often turn the tables on them by invoking the expertise they've achieved from focusing on very specific tasks.

In either circumstance, micromanagement numbs the brains and kills the spirits of the people whose autonomy is being usurped.

2. Unreliable people disappear and play hard-to-find. This is very common and very destructive. The usual excuse for playing hard-to-get is that someone is just too busy to get back to you. But when good managers don't have time to respond, they tell you right away. It takes seconds, and nobody feels slighted.

It usually doesn't help to confront the person, because they probably won't give you a genuine, transparent response. We're all busy—that's why they call it bus-i-ness—but anybody who hides behind that excuse is looking for ways to stay out of situations they don't understand.

3. Unreliable people have chronic punctuality problems. They miss planes, are late for everything from lunch to a project completion, and act as if it makes them very important—rather than a very big pain in the ass.

This is a tell of both incompetence *and* lack of diligence, a kiss of death for reliability. Competent people manage their time. Diligent people manage it even when it's almost unmanageable. Either way, you can rely on them to get something done.

4. Unreliable people grab the credit of others. These people don't have much of a work ethic, or they wouldn't need to pretend they did the work of others. For example, about a hundred agents had a hand in the famous femme fatale spy case of Anna Chapman, and I've met dozens of them, and most of them took almost full credit for it.

This happens most among relatively small teams—when the rest of the team isn't around—because there are fewer people to confront.

Some people do this even when they've achieved their *own* assignment, and have been *rewarded* for it. These are the scary people, because they have a compulsive need to steal. They are, in effect, the kleptomaniacs of intellectual property.

5. Unreliable people are frequently careless about appearance and physical presentation.

This doesn't apply to people who sincerely believe they are dressing appropriately—such as a techie in a hoodie.

It applies to people who don't even try. It's a sign of disrespect: for you and, more important, for themselves and their work. They don't think they're doing well, so they act it out in an indirect, sublimated way. Their sloppy presentation is self-destructive, and you don't want to become collateral damage.

This is a subtle tell, because the people who do it usually *say* they're reliable, and are unaware that they're actually revealing their disappointment in themselves.

Instead of dealing with that painful issue in a forthright way—which would open them to direct criticism—they come to work in sloppy or dirty clothes, their hygiene isn't great, they litter, their office is a mess, they lose things, they have poor health habits, or they drive a dirty car.

You don't need to be Freud to see that these shortcomings subconsciously mirror their self-perception.

What they *think* they're saying: "I'm like Einstein—a scatter-brained genius!"

6. Unreliable people depend on *others* to fix their problems. This is another good example of fear disguised as arrogance.

People are supposed to feel reliable *themselves,* and act accordingly. That doesn't mean that everybody can fix everything, but some people just don't feel confident or energetic enough to finish something on their own.

When people lack a bedrock sense of self-sufficiency, they're prone to handing off problems without even *trying* to solve them.

If someone appears to overuse your various support systems, it may be the tip of an iceberg of unreliability.

7. Unreliable people have a hard time picking up new concepts. That doesn't mean they're dumb. It means their range of competence is narrow, and they haven't done much to broaden it.

The FBI, like most large organizations, offers training in many areas, so when someone lacks multiple certifications, it's an indication that they don't believe in their own competence, or that they lack the diligence to care.

Most people who have a multitude of limitations have limited themselves—and if you vest your success in them, you may be limiting yourself, too.

8. Unreliable people don't keep adequate records. This is one of those traits that escapes the attention of many managers, because in our fast-forward world, records are often perceived as ancient history.

Bad record keeping also creates the possibility that someone is hiding things.

One of the most damaging aspects of this tell is bad note-taking by people in meetings, conferences, and teleconferences. By the time the damage from this surfaces, it can usually be blamed on many different issues, or on other people.

Good notes are a great tell of someone's ability and desire to excel, because they most often reflect the thoughts of *other* people—not just oneself.

Bad note-taking connotes indifference to the thoughts and opinions of those talking, and when it's done in person, it can signify a sense of superiority.

The monstrous dictator Joseph Stalin was known for taking copious notes—and only much later was it revealed that most of them were just doodles.

9. Unreliable people are more involved in planning than action. Planning is great, but it's just the beginning of a project. That should be obvious, but it isn't, especially among people with limited attention spans.

These people often lose interest in a project when its initial aura of excitement fades. They want somebody else to come in and do the grunt work of execution and maintenance.

People who avoid the routine chores of a project sometimes act as if they're simply adept at delegating responsibility, but they're more likely to just be scattered and impulsive.

A tell behind this tell is that the people who shirk responsibility typically don't document their work. That gives them the opportunity to bail on failures.

When I first joined the Bureau, I was encouraged to write down my actions in regular reports as my operations unfolded, because that was the best way to document success or failure. My supervisor's mantra was, "If you didn't write it, you didn't do it."

I've stuck with that system ever since, and I insist on it in the teams I run.

10. Unreliable people don't take their own mistakes seriously. They try to escape blame through various strategies—blaming others, claiming they were not warned about the cause of the mistake, or doctoring details to make the mistake look inevitable.

Another very common reaction is to just minimize the mistake. If they put a decimal point in the wrong place and it costs the company a thousand dollars, they see it as nothing more than a typo, or a small loss for a big company. It's common for people to be too critical of themselves, but also common to not be critical enough.

Irresponsible people also often redefine their mistakes as learning experiences that were actually fortuitous.

These were the negative tells that I looked for in my assessment of George. I found some of them, but also found some positive tells, such as him admitting that he'd made a couple of mistakes.

It's always nice when leaders admit their mistakes, but it's nicer when they don't make them.

September 2018
Ahead of the Action

One month in, I loved working on the drone team, and felt like a reliable teammate. For me, it was the perfect mix of aeronautical technology and manpower management—two of my comfort zones—and most of the time I felt like I was in front of the action, moving at my own pace, a step or two ahead of real time. That's a magical, almost metaphysical time frame—familiar territory for reliable people—that feels great and makes things happen.

In the luxurious flow of that feeling, created by confidence and determination, you feel like you can actually see the future, for a very prosaic reason: You're helping to create it. Most of what you do feels familiar and predictable, and you can greet each new day like an old friend.

The power of feeling reliable—magnified exponentially by your own reliance on the people around you—comes naturally to the best managers, and they pass the feeling on to the team, creating a culture of excellence, and adherence to best practices.

It didn't come naturally to me—I had to sweat for it, but that was fine, because when I feel like I'm creating my own future, work *replenishes* my energy, instead of draining it, and good ideas seem to arrive right on schedule as my vigor and sense of accomplishment builds.

So I was in a good mood when I arrived at George's office unannounced. I hardly ever make surprise appearances, but I was having a hard time connecting with him, and wanted to share an idea: a practical way to help control and predict the criminal use of drones domestically.

Thus far, the government had tried to limit access to drones at the sourcing stage—retail sales—similarly to guns and other munitions. But I'd been thinking about the 9/11 attack and how the terrorists had trained at U.S. aviation schools. Shortly before the attack, an FBI agent had alerted the Bureau about this training, and we were in the preliminary stages of identifying the eventual hijackers, and canvassing all American aviation schools about possible use of their training programs by terrorists. We were a step too late.

Why not do it right this time? Why not get in touch with all the drone training programs in the country now and ask them to report suspicious behavior? That strategy could give us a viable choke point at the intersection of terrorists and training.

George liked the idea, even though it would, by definition, be a people-driven operation. He promised me he'd look into it after he caught up on some paperwork.

I didn't see the need to wait, but he was the boss. So I dropped it and asked him about the expert I had previously recommended to him. I had been talking to the guy on a regular basis and knew that George hadn't contacted him.

"Don't worry," George said. "It's in the works." But I knew it wasn't, and it made me uneasy. The expert had two PhDs from Johns Hopkins and was a lifetime military man. We *really* needed him—and his colleagues—because George was in charge of arranging for speakers, and he hadn't mentioned finding any.

George was getting fidgety, and let me know that I was intruding, with his body language: quick glances at the papers on his desk and the clock on the wall, with facial expressions of impatience. But he was too polite to say anything—unless passive-aggressive nonverbals say something: which they *do.*

He changed the subject to some of his logistical concerns—funding, coordination, time lines. Good move: for getting me to *leave.* He knew those details didn't involve me.

I was getting the feeling that he felt threatened by me, as a peer with equal authority. That was not good. The last person you ever want to pose a threat to is your team leader, for the obvious reason: You can get kicked off the team—or even fired from the organization—for a strictly personal reason that will never be admitted.

That happens about a million times a day in America, and I often see the behavior that's revealed by the fear it causes.

America is one of the safest countries in the world—but also one of the most fearful. Its wealth is mirrored by an equal fear of losing it. There is no apparent middle ground remaining in this country, and the center, as they say, will not hold.

I fear fear. It's the *real* root of all evil, and it's commonly embodied by the boring, trivial cuts and jabs of office politics and petty grievances that lie in the realm of aggression that philosopher Hannah

Arendt called "the banality of evil." I'm not saying George was evil. I'm simply stating the obvious: What we do in our lives affects others, and if we don't consciously try to affect people in a positive way, our actions can easily cause a spiral of hurt that gets worse every day.

What George had done had already negated the three signs of trust he'd displayed when I first met him, indicating, once more, that when situations change, people change.

I still liked George, but was starting to think he was just clueless when it came to people, and was therefore not competent to fulfill his role. He could have compensated for his lack of competence by being very diligent—or just asking for help—but it wasn't happening.

When I got up to leave, though, he was genuinely warm. That was the scary part. He meant well, but he was in the vast herd of humanity that means well but just can't do what you need them to, and often aren't even willing to try.

So I didn't know if I could trust him anymore—at least, not with this project, nor my own future.

TEN POSITIVE TELLS FOR RELIABILITY
(COMPETENCE PLUS DILIGENCE)

1. Reliable people carry themselves with genuine confidence. It's fairly easy to fake confidence, so behavioral analysts have learned how to identify true, unforced confidence. People who have it don't brag, don't make excuses, take their jobs more seriously than themselves, and get things done.

They're calm, polite, succinct, receptive, rational, and reliable. All of that shows in their nonverbals, the language they use, the relationships they have, their patterns of behavior, and their focus on long-term goals.

One study of top-tier managers showed that a display of genuine confidence was a key element in their success. And it was present in them *before* their success. The study also confirmed the phenomenon called "erotic capital"—the confidence enjoyed by people who are notably attractive and have translated that into worldly success.

My takeaway: Forget about fake-it-till-you-make-it. Instead, try *feel*-it-till-you-make-it, focusing on the *positive qualities you already have.*

I call this self-selected, legitimate feeling "quantifiable confidence," and I've found that most people have enough positive attributes to sincerely project confidence—if they try.

2. Reliable people speak with specifics. They bring communication instead of confusion to a conversation. They're clear, concise, memorable, and motivational—in accord with Brockman's dictum—and their words create charisma. The things they say in important professional conversations, and in presentations, stand out in a society of big talkers who try to prove their worth with circular talk, cutesy jargon, excessive modifiers, and political correctness so thick it's mind-numbing.

The people you trust and admire the most don't talk like that.

Most of us know instinctually not to trust big talkers, because we don't know where they stand, or even understand what they've said. That makes them unpredictable, and therefore untrustworthy—and vice versa.

3. Reliable people are transparent about their weaknesses and mistakes. They don't repackage their failures as successes. They don't pretend that their weak points have become their strengths. They're not defensive.

Most of us love working with people like this, because their strengths and weaknesses are obvious, which is pure gold for predictability.

Reliable people don't leave you with that hollow feeling you get when an insecure person talks. Most of the time, you can tell that insecure people don't even know that they're being defensive. They think they're just putting their best foot forward.

The rest of us think they're hiding something, and we often underestimate how egregious it actually is.

4. Reliable people welcome tough jobs and hard deadlines. Heavy lifting gives reliable people the welcome opportunity to show others what they can do. These people are self-aware enough to know they're reliable, and they like to demonstrate it.

They're also realistic enough to know that they need to keep proving themselves.

Reliable people tend to get lost in the flow state that accompanies focus, selflessness, and intensity, and they're aware of the fact that hard work can be a form of meditation.

Also, when reliable people are held accountable, it generally just reveals how well they've done—so why *shouldn't* they like it?

5. Reliable people hit the ground running and then speed up. People who are competent and diligent are able to do their work quickly, because they know the processes, have the tools to get it done, and feel a personal sense of urgency.

For the *most* diligent people, one of the rewards of working fast is finishing first, and then helping others. It makes them feel good—and look good.

Work needs to be done *well*, of course, but speed always counts. It helps organizations outrun their competitors, it attracts other reliable people, it keeps people sharp, it makes time move quickly, it sets a good example, it saves the company money, and it usually becomes the new normal.

Fast is good.

A quick, high-quality turnaround on a project is one of the best objective measurements of reliability. The clock doesn't lie.

6. Reliable people are inquisitive. Curiosity is the spark that lights the fire of learning, and is also the soul of creativity.

Reliable people have a multitude of questions about their own job, other jobs, and the industry as a whole. The knowledge they accumulate empowers them to refine their work processes to a state of optimal efficiency.

As a rule, people who don't ask questions are either uninterested in their work, or are afraid that their questions will make them look unsure or incompetent.

When reliable people are being interviewed for a job, they often have as many questions as answers. They're not desperate, and want to work in a place where they'll be happy and satisfied. So they ask—politely and transparently—about scheduling, upward mobility, benefits, company culture, the physical work environment, and other issues that will contribute to their contentment and security.

They also want to know about you and your associates, because they're seeking a situation of mutual vesting. So once again we see the interlocking nature of our six signs for predicting people.

7. Reliable people accept blame graciously. They know that nobody's perfect, including them. As a rule, the only people who pretend to be perfect are those who aren't even very good at what they do, and try to hide their insecurity behind a facade of perfectionism.

But that just makes things worse, because being a perfectionist doesn't make a person feel perfect—since nobody's perfect. Instead, it makes them feel even more inadequate.

Reliable people rarely get ruffled when somebody calls them out, because they almost always have a deep reservoir of goodwill, and know they'll live to fight another day. They approach it as just another learning experience.

8. Reliable people don't measure their contributions by their sacrifices, but by their productivity. They don't talk about how hard something was, unless there's a practical reason to mention it. They don't complain about giving up vacation time, or meeting with people they'd rather avoid, or taking on projects that don't interest them.

As far as they're concerned, those are *their* problems, and they know you have your own.

Many reliable people believe in working smarter, not harder—but most of them believe in working smarter *and* harder.

They keep track of their achievements, but just for their own sense of satisfaction, and if they've gotten certificates or plaques, you've probably never seen them.

9. Reliable people's nonverbals remain stable, and even positive, during times of stress and strain. Hard times are the best measure of a person's competence and diligence, and during hard times, nonverbal behaviors are even more revealing than what people say, write, and do, because nonverbals are harder to hide, and harder to fake.

In times of trouble, most of us can refrain from overt acts of bad behavior, such as bullying, snapping at people, or feuding with others. In most workplaces these days, that's simply expected, and demanded.

But highly reliable people are also able to refrain from physical responses to stress that are *seemingly ingrained and uncontrollable*, such as sweating, muscle tension, hyperventilation, an upset stomach, pacing, or cold hands and feet. It's not easy. Those responses are all governed by the fight-flight-freeze mechanism of the autonomic nervous system, and are therefore hard to control.

But reliable people can do that, because even in a crisis, they still feel largely in control of themselves and their responses. They're calm, reasonable, physically comfortable, and capable of focus.

Their reaction is not based upon delusions of indestructability. They face the same consequences as everyone else, but they're confident that they'll weather the storm—and they usually do.

One ironic reason they succeed is because they don't feel as if they *need* to. They don't like losing, but they don't measure themselves by wins and losses. They measure themselves by their competence and diligence: They do their best and let the chips fall.

10. Reliable people don't have enemies. They don't need to. People with enemies are usually their *own* best enemy—because of self-doubt—and their enemies are just surrogates for themselves. If you're competent and diligent, it's hard to blame yourself for losing a battle. You did the best you could. End of drama.

When you're no longer fixated on enemies, they're gone, but the lesson of their incursion into your life remains. You can move on with your life.

October 2018

The drone conference was only a month away, and George was losing what little faith in him that I still had. He didn't have the skills, aptitude, training, or temperament to run a team that was only partly focused on technology.

It was not his fault. He was just a fish out of water.

I had given him many opportunities to display some of the tells of reliability, but he didn't come through on most of them. The tells of positive behavior that he *failed* to fulfill included: not speaking in specifics at meetings (Positive Tell #2), not being transparent about his weaknesses (Positive Tell #3), not asking many questions (Positive Tell #6), not making his deadlines (Positive Tell #5), and refusing to take responsibility when problems were pointed out (Positive Tell #7).

He'd also been weak in so many other tells—and the data points supporting them—that I'd shifted my perspective to one of distrust and disaffiliation.

That wasn't unusual. I've chosen *not* to ally myself with many people, many times, because even though I try to trust people, I often deal with people who don't live up to it. It's hardly ever because they're rotten people. It's just that they display too many signs of alienation and unpredictability to make me feel comfortable.

George had already displayed several objective, evidence-based tells of distrust. He'd driven me crazy with his tendency to be unavailable (Negative Tell #2), and even when I was able to pin him down on an appointment, he was chronically late (Negative Tell #3). At our meetings, he micromanaged, without providing any value-added services (Negative Tell #1).

I'd tried hard to be a resource for his success, and had not given up on him easily. But this had dragged on too long.

I wanted to resign from the task force, but I'd never quit a major assignment in my life. And if I did, and it triggered other resignations, it would be a significant black mark on George's career. It could also stall America's response to the drone threat.

So late in the summer I gave George a last chance to get his ass in gear and call the expert I'd recommended, and to find out if his colleagues would speak. George forgot, so I gave him *another* last chance—and that brought me from summer to autumn, and led to his *last* last chance. I was still optimistic—because I hang on to that perspective like a bulldog—but also realistic, because I value rationality as much as optimism.

"Robin, my friend!" George said when I showed up at his office, again unexpectedly. "Good to see you!" He meant it. I'd told him the week before that if he didn't reach out to the expert I'd found, I would take it into my own hands, and personally deliver the good news—if there was good news.

I'd gotten the expert's consent, as well as that of his colleagues, and was ready to deliver the good news. But at this point I was worried that the whole project had drifted into chaos.

When I saw George's desk, it reinforced my distrust of his organizational skills. It looked like somebody had just emptied a wastebasket on it. I saw one document in which a banana was apparently serving as a bookmark. It was hard not to stare at it (Negative Tell #5).

I handed George some papers from the expert, including a rough outline of the keynote address, and a list of his colleagues who had also agreed to speak. I was hoping some of them could be used as consultants and become part of the permanent national security structure.

Others, I thought, might become confidential human sources in the project I had proposed: gathering information at drone flight schools.

"Recognize any names?" I asked him. Some of the people were very prominent in the area of drone regulation. I'd met one of them at a training course, along with some producers from ABC News.

George shook his head. It was fairly obvious that he hadn't become conversant on the issue yet (Negative Tell #7), probably because he was still focused on logistics and finance. It didn't surprise me. At this point, nothing could.

I pointed at the top four names on a list of potential speakers. "Want a quick rundown on these guys?" I asked.

"Absolutely."

I started, but quickly stopped. He wasn't taking any notes (Negative Tell #8), and I wasn't going to waste more of my time. I knew then that this relationship was over.

"You don't seem super interested in this part of the project," I said, as gently as possible, because I don't have enemies, and want to keep it that way.

"I'm interested," he protested, "but I've got people who can take care of that kind of thing. Won't be a problem!" (Negative Tell #9.) At this point, I just wanted out.

"Robin," he said, "you're doing a terrific job. But I think you're overestimating some problems and underestimating others."

I nodded in agreement—to whatever *that* meant—for the sake of gracious closure.

"I probably should have mentioned this," he said, "but I got some people of my own to speak."

I was wrong. He *could* surprise me.

"But maybe I could squeeze your guy into a fifteen-minute slot," he said. "I wouldn't want to insult him."

No, not much!

"I'll ask him about that," I said.

But that wasn't going to happen. What did happen was that I called up the expert, apologized profusely, and told him the truth, the whole truth, and nothing but.

And by the end of that call, I had another solid, trust-based relationship with one of the most stable and predictable people I've ever known.

I resigned so quietly from the task force that I hardly noticed it myself.

I was not done with the issue. It needed work, and still does. But I knew that there was a better place for me.

The hard part of that was not getting there. The hard part was knowing it had to be.

DEBRIEFING

CHAPTER 5:
"KNOW WHO TO GO TO"

SIGN #3: RELIABILITY

Key Quote: "You can love someone with all your heart and trust them with your deepest secrets, but there are countless areas in which relying upon that same person would be not just impossible, but insane."

Key Message: Reliability is virtually synonymous with positive behavior, and requires a combination of competence and diligence.

THE TAKEAWAYS

Competence: The skills, knowledge, and experience that a task requires.

1. Lack of competence—and the lack of ability to quickly become competent—is typically a dealbreaker for predicting success at a task.
2. Competence can generally be accurately measured.
3. Most people are competent in a relatively small number of difficult professional tasks.

Diligence: The character qualities—such as drive, self-responsibility, and a strong work ethic—that turn competence into action and completion.

1. Virtually anyone, with enough effort, can be diligent. But diligence is harder to measure than competence, and is easier to fake.
2. Approximately 50 percent of all people lack diligence, according to behavioral science polls.
3. Lack of diligence destroys reliability through absenteeism, poor productivity, apathy, lethargy, and negativity.

Ten Positive Tells for Reliability (Competence Plus Diligence)

1. They are genuinely confident for the obvious reason: They know what they're doing.
2. They speak with specifics: clear, concise, memorable, motivational (C^2M^2).
3. They're transparent about mistakes and weaknesses. No sad stories.
4. They welcome difficulties and deadlines. They know that hard can be fun.
5. They work fast, finish first, and know that time is money.
6. They're inquisitive. That's worth its weight in platinum. Questions prevent problems.

7. They accept responsibility—never with excuses, but sometimes with reasons.

8. They're productive. They don't watch the clock—they watch their production.

9. They display comfortable nonverbals during hard tasks.

10. They don't hold grudges and don't seek revenge.

Ten Negative Tells for Reliability (Competence Plus Diligence)

1. They micromanage, without really helping.

2. They're hard to contact—on purpose.

3. They're chronically late: a nasty combo of lack of diligence *and* competence.

4. They grab credit, often so surreptitiously that they get away with it.

5. They have a careless physical presentation: sloppy, dirty, messy.

6. They make others solve the hardest problems.

7. They learn slowly. They don't care.

8. They're careless with record keeping—a great way to hide things. Or they're just lazy.

9. They like planning far more than action. It's easier.

10. They don't take their mistakes seriously. Sometimes they're not even aware of them.

6

DETERMINE THE DEALBREAKERS

Sign #4: ACTIONS

Does this person consistently demonstrate patterns of positive behavior?

New York, 2003
Rule Number One

After my supervisor rejected my most recent proposal for an operation, I asked Jesse, "Do you think there's *anybody* around here who believes in me?"

I didn't know what to do, or even how to act.

I felt free to vent my disturbed state of mind around Jesse because I knew he wouldn't get caught up in my emotion. He'd think it through and help me find a new supervisor, or a better approach to my current one. But I didn't expect an instant answer, because he was too smart to offer any thoughts at all until he knew exactly what my situation was—stripped of its histrionics—and how I was *really* feeling, once I'd broken free of the debris from my pity party.

So Jesse started applying the behavioral science technique of asking nonjudgmental, rational questions, called "discovery questions," which are intended to lead people—rather than push them—toward their own inner wisdom and bedrock reality, beneath their layers of defensiveness, conjecture, and insecurity.

All these layers are founded in fear, but have different names—including perfectionism, suspicion, or status seeking—and each offers a different form of fiction.

The only antidote for them is to return to realistic thought, but that's not as hard as it sounds, because reality is rarely as threatening as the various scenarios we conjure in our brain's fear center, during life's darkest hours.

Jesse, though, thought life could be great *if people would just see it as it really is.* So he never settled for just telling people what they wanted to hear, and he didn't take the lazy route of telling them what *he* would do in their situation. People usually tune that out, because it's not specifically about *them*, and can come off as condescending.

He just listened carefully enough to get into people's heads, and see what was best for them from their *own* perspective. That alone was of supreme value, because people love to be understood, even more than they love someone agreeing with them. When people calm down, he found, they can usually be trusted to do what's in their own best interests—as *they* perceive them.

By the time Jesse was done, people would usually know not only how they really felt, but also what they really *thought.*

Those two conditions should go together, but they often don't. Feelings are almost always attached to thoughts, but the emotions they create can be so illusory and ephemeral that rational thoughts evaporate.

In contrast, the durable product of cognitive thought—far more than feelings—is *the primary predictor of what rational people will do.* Because, of course, people usually do what they think is in their own best interests.

Knowing what's good for you may sound easy, but I've long believed that it's the hardest element to isolate in the often awkward intersection of thought and emotion. Unfortunately, when human beings start thinking about what's best for them, they kid themselves a lot. We're often too dreamy, and call it optimism, or too fearful, and call it prudence. Then we grab an option, tack it onto the problem, and abandon rational management of the situation.

Then, when Plan A doesn't work, people often just sink deeper into distrust of not only those around them, but also themselves. That's when we start screwing ourselves up.

The danger of pervasive doubt and alienation may seem obvious to you, but an astonishing number of people just don't get it—and possibly never will—because distrust, like other forms of self-imposed isolation, is a *self-perpetuating* character flaw.

When wary people fail to find an accurate way to predict the actions of those around them, they usually don't feel safe enough to go ahead and do what's best for themselves. Some of them are afraid they'll be seen as selfish, controlling, or incompetent, and others are just tired of being burned by people they once thought were allies.

Even more distressing, millions of people *do* know what's in their own best interests—and by extension, the best interests of their families, friends, and colleagues—but *still* surrender their own precious peace of mind to unfounded fears, temptations, and pressures.

When that happens, they usually fail to act on the simple but sacred honor of doing what's best for themselves and for those closest to them. Often as not, these people do it again and again, thinking that their sacrifices will save the world—or at least *them*—if only the world would come to its senses, and revolve around them.

I'm not judging this behavior, because most people make these sacrifices with a good heart. But when it doesn't work, it can harden their hearts, kill their spirits, and exhaust their bodies and minds. At that point, they need someone to help them go back to square one and make sure they still want the goals that once seemed so important.

Deciding what you want most, though, is rarely as simple as doing whatever you feel like doing. Whatever you do usually affects the people around you, and if what you do hurts them, you'll probably create an enemy, or at least get a negative reaction. Then things get really difficult. That's why discovery questions can be so effective. These questions are general and sincere, and are not the *rhetorical* questions that manipulative people ask. Their purpose is to point the way to rational action. Common discovery questions that fit most problems are: What's the worst-case scenario? Who might not like it? What will they do? What have I tried so far? Did those actions lead to an ultimate goal, or just an immediate goal? Have other people tried to help? What actions might make things worse?

Jesse asked me a discovery question embedded in a sincere compliment that was too flattering to reject: "Who around here could not trust *you,* Robin?"

"My supervisor. And his supervisor."

"Why do you think that?"

"They keep rejecting my operations. Including the current one."

"What's their reasoning?"

"Too risky."

After ten or twenty simple, straightforward questions, he knew my full context—which, as I've mentioned, consists of a rational, informed understanding of the *person* plus the *situation.*

"You've already done the best possible thing," Jesse said.

"I haven't done *anything.*"

"Right! That might feel passive to you, but it's a real aggressive way to outsmart your emotions—especially when you're pissed off or scared. That emotional nonsense is like the fog of war. You've gotta let it lift before you do something. *Then* you make your move. It takes discipline to wait. But Rule Number One is: Don't f**k yourself up. Leave that to other people. They're not as good at it as you are. You're *your own best enemy.*"

"It's good to be the best at something," I said.

He laughed. Humor comes easily when you can see the big picture.

He was lost in thought for a couple of minutes.

Then he said, "You need a new supervisor. And I already know the guy. You do, too. Jack! Jack Johnson. We can create a new operation and invite Jack *and* your current supervisor to be in it, and you'll get the best of both worlds."

Jack, as you may remember, was the supervisor who'd wrangled the bureaucracy into approving my first operation with Annan, which Jesse sometimes referred to as "preventing World War III," occasionally quite seriously.

"Jack's a good guy," I said, "but he wouldn't let me work the Annan operation unless I did it with you. Why do you think he'd have faith in me now?"

"First of all, because he *did* give you the operation," Jesse said. "Never overlook the obvious. And the only reason he had me tag along wasn't because he didn't trust you. It was because he didn't trust his own supervisor. He was working for a low-risk/no-risk guy at HQ and knew he'd have to attach a senior agent to get the Yes. But he's perfect for you, because his motto is *Feed the Beast:* Keep supplying headquarters with operations, even when they're risky. He's running his own ops now, and he's still mission-first, not career-first. He rocks the boat and doesn't look for scapegoats. But the supervisors trust him, because he sticks to his core values, and that makes him very predictable: a known commodity. Which makes *them* look brilliant."

"So he'll be cool with this new thing?"

He nodded. "Jack makes it look easy to feed the beast. He gets a read on people from what they say; then he cross-checks it with open sources, preferably with numbers. By then he's a mind reader. He does it with his supervisors, and he'll do it with you."

"Okay," I said, somewhat tentatively.

"Oh, plus—he's hit lotto eighteen times."

Sold!

Within a week, Jack had reengineered my operation, softening the risks that management had seen, but still keeping me as the lead agent—a brilliant bureaucratic feat that kept everyone happy, including me. He remembered me well from the prior operation, and knowing my past patterns of behavior played a critical role in his willingness to trust me in this new role.

Actions matter. More than anything else. For good or ill, it's your actions that define you, much more obviously and accurately than what you say or how you feel.

Troublesome words and feelings come and go, but deals die when bad things actually occur, in the real world, and in real time.

More than any other form of self-expression, actions are viable *deal-breakers*. They're not just a thought. They're *what happens.*

When they happen can also make a big difference. Past actions don't always affect the present, but current actions usually do.

The operation I wanted to run would, I thought, result in major actions at the international level. Jesse liked it, I liked it, and Jack liked it. The prior rejections suddenly looked like the screwups of timid bureaucrats, so the other supervisor went along.

The mission was to recruit a Russian target who was a former Soviet general, with the help of an American CHS who'd been a prominent marine colonel. They were both public figures, and the patterns of their past and current behaviors were largely open-source information. I'd only talked to the colonel briefly, and had never spoken to the Russian, but I already felt as if I knew both of them well.

Not incidentally, the target was now a major player in Russian-American diplomacy. Recruiting him, at a time when Vladimir Putin was beginning to look like a modern-day czar, would be like hitting Powerball lotto.

Best of all, the general and the colonel were old friends. Now, you tell me: How could a setup like that *ever* get rejected?

The Power of Character

What people do—including what they've done consistently in the past—greatly heightens their predictability, because it reveals the rock-hard core of their character, consisting of their primary principles and values.

Because many different principles and values compose character, most people consider some elements of character to be more important than others, and they hold those qualities closest. For example, some people might be more concerned about being honest than being humble, or more dedicated to being kind than being authentic.

I always try to get a read on the values that people hold dear to their hearts—their core values—because they're a window into someone's inner self, and are the traits most likely to influence people, and to remain steadfast even when circumstances change.

Quite often, a person's character is forged by the philosophical and moral codes that they adopted many years earlier, often in adolescence or early adulthood, as they created their own unique codes of character.

In a sense, therefore, what people will do has already been determined by choices they made long ago. As the preeminent Stoic philosopher Epictetus said, "It is your own convictions that compel you: that is, choice compels choice." That's why it's important to evaluate people by the entirety of their lives, in addition to how they've behaved in the more recent past. To a large extent, we become what we have long intended to become.

Placing importance on character is very consistent with the concept that emotionally healthy people usually do what they believe is in their own best interests, because someone's best interests almost always include adhering to their own codes of conduct. When they violate them, they usually feel guilty and regretful, and fear that their violations will not only stunt their personal growth and self-esteem, but also their acceptance by others. This attachment to character makes people much easier to predict, and therefore easier to trust with your own fate.

Codes of morality also often come from various religions and philosophies, and most of them include some qualities of good character that are virtually universal. These include honesty, loyalty, kindness, humility, respect, and integrity.

The nobility of these qualities is practically inarguable. Therefore, they are the primary and sometimes sole factors that people consider when they assess trust. Some people simplify the process by trusting someone based only upon their particular religion—especially if they share it—but that's risky, because merely belonging to a particular faith does not automatically grant good character. Even so, looking for these bedrock qualities in other people is one of those fundamental, basic acts that allow us to accurately evaluate them, and assign a realistic reputation to them. Despite all its shortcomings, it's one of the valid metrics for assessing trust and predicting what people will do.

As always, though, in the soft science of behaviorism, this rule is rife with exceptions and contradictions. Human behavior always comes back to two hard truths: 1) we're only human, and 2) nobody is perfect. Rules, therefore, are only as perfect as the people who apply them, and character can be surprisingly malleable, especially when it's not in the category of a *core* character.

Behavioral studies indicate that people with impeccable behavior in the past often fall short of their prior good behavior. Even though people don't change their core personality very often, they certainly behave differently from time to time, in ways that seem almost random, unless you pay close attention to them. If you do, you often find that they think their environment has changed and that they need to adjust. That can happen often, and quickly, because most environments are in a constant state of flux.

The changes that affect character most, as I've mentioned, are threats and temptations, which sometimes occur simultaneously.

Past patterns of honesty and fairness have also been shown to crumble when people believe that they can indulge in their actions anonymously, or remain free from consequences.

We see that happen repeatedly in two of the professions that are magnets for power: politics and business management. This common phenomenon is often called the "power paradox."

Conversely, people who know that they will be held responsible for their actions are those who are most likely to adhere to their past patterns of positive behavior. But if the situation changes, they might, too. That phenomenon seems to be somewhat common among the trusted people who become embezzlers, or among attorneys who know how to skirt the law.

Another frequently cited element of good character is loyalty, but this is one more moral positive that may simply be a matter of expedience.

A history of honesty is usually considered one of the most valuable indicators of strong character and trustworthiness, but honesty sounds far simpler than it is. Many professional people become adept at telling the truth, but rarely the whole truth.

Honesty can also be used as a weapon, especially when someone delivers an insult prefaced by the phrase, "I'm just being honest."

The same factors that complicate honesty also obscure integrity. Integrity is a fine quality, but it, too, can become twisted to the point that it becomes destructive. People often wield the tool of integrity to attack people they oppose.

Authenticity, too, is a precious quality, but negative aspects of one's character can be quite authentic, and still be inappropriate or even indefensible.

Another gray area of authenticity occurs when people take out their anger on others by saying that they're just "being themselves" or "calling it like they see it."

Despite all these incursions on character, though, most people try extremely hard to adhere to their core, central values.

The takeaway: Patterns of behavior, especially over a long period of time, define people's character, and *character counts*—even as an imperfect measure. That's why action is one of only six signs of sizing people up.

So be generous to people who may have been coerced or otherwise dragged into questionable behavior. But be careful. And be just as careful of people who have sterling reputations.

Doveryai no Proveryai!

TEN NEGATIVE TELLS FOR PATTERNS OF ACTIONS

1. People are not fully transparent about their pasts. Many people have a "secret spot": an event or act that they try to hide, by ignoring part of their work history, or by skating past certain questions in their initial job interviews, or in general conversations.

The degree of gaps in time and information generally indicates the importance of the secret spot, and people with significant secrets just aren't predictable enough to be trustworthy.

If they're open about it, though, that's different. Transparency solves innumerable problems of prediction.

2. People treat those with power better than those without it.

There is only one "real" side to this kind of person: the rude one. Bad behavior is almost always controllable, if the person *wants* to control it. So sucking up to the boss doesn't count.

Be careful of these people, because sycophants are dangerous to everyone they work with. Their behavior is frequently used to become the boss's pet, and they'll throw you to the wolves, and never think twice about it.

3. People have gaps or exaggerations on their résumés. It sounds like a dealbreaker, but sometimes it's not.

Business culture, for good or ill, now often tolerates a modest degree of gold-plating, so some applicants feel that their mild misstatements amount to little more than putting their best foot forward.

Two things control the fib: the *degree* of misinformation, and how the person *responds* to being questioned about their misstatement. If they're okay on one or both, give them a break. But keep your eye on them.

4. People regard their competitors as enemies, and attack them whenever possible. Dealbreaker. This pattern of behavior appeals to a specific type of gung-ho, take-no-prisoners operator. It can be seductive, because there is a hard edge to business that must be faced. But it's juvenile behavior that they should have outgrown. Competition does not demand anger.

The same people might soon be taking out their anger on you. For innately hostile people, it's all about control.

Find people who have friends throughout the industry.

5. People have a history of irregular behavior patterns in their personal lives. This could include multiple divorces, family feuds, minor legal or ethical matters, or numerous failed friendships. These are the kinds of nonwork issues, once hidden from employers, that are now on full display on social media.

Everybody has problems, but usually just troublemakers have lots of them. That's often an indicator of wholesale unpredictability. Take a pass.

6. You feel like you don't know someone, even after close, prolonged contact. It may not reflect their core personal qualities at all—but it still leaves you with a lack of information. And information—not intuition, and not affection—is the foundation of all predictability.

Ask them specific questions that are neither prying nor accusatory. If you can't get straight answers, you'll never really know what makes them tick.

It's a dangerous situation—and could bring unwanted surprises.

7. People are tight-lipped about past colleagues. What are they hiding? Whatever it is, it's keeping you from really knowing them—and that's a dealbreaker.

Predicting people is all about *knowing them.*

If they don't want you to know what other people think about them, you'll never know what to expect.

Maybe they don't want to talk about their former colleagues because they don't trust them. But that's *your* call, not theirs.

8. People are critical about their colleagues' personal lives. It's usually irrelevant. And it's creepy. It's especially creepy when they criticize people who've left the company.

You can't help but wonder what they'll say about you someday.

You need to align yourself with people who stick to *facts*—not feelings, not hearsay—and who know what matters and what doesn't.

Even if what they're saying is interesting, don't feed into it. Anybody can tell a good story, but sometimes that's all it is: a *story*. Don't be a sucker for it.

9. A person's behavior is often inconsistent. Another dealbreaker. This is bad-news behavior, since consistency creates predictability, and predictability creates trust and effectiveness.

Inconsistency, and the drama it creates, sometimes has a certain romantic, devil-may-care panache to it, but it's the worst possible trait at crunch time. In a crisis, it can be the kiss of death.

10. It's hard for someone to accept responsibility, especially for major mistakes. This is so common—and so sad—because it almost *never* works. When was the last time you saw somebody actually beat the rap by stonewalling?

This behavior is founded in insecurity, though, so it can be addressed, and often reversed, by assuring people of their security and cultivating a blame-free culture around them.

But when people cling to their defensiveness after you do your best to make them feel safe and appreciated, be careful. They don't trust you, so you can't trust them.

New York, 2003
Feed the Beast

When Jack gave me the go-ahead on my diplomatic operation, I started surveillance of the Russian general, looking for patterns of behavior that would add to our understanding of his character and his past. It would give us an update on his current priorities, reveal the optimal environment in which to approach him, and provide us with a good conversation starter.

I was hoping that he realized that his own future, and that of his family, was now aligned more with the United States, and the West in general, than with Putin and his oligarchs. I thought he'd see it that way—but, as always, what I thought came from my *own* context, and his was quite different. We wouldn't know how he felt until we launched the operation—or, as we put it, bought our lotto ticket. You can't win if you don't play.

In all honesty, the operation wasn't likely to succeed. *Most* of our operations didn't hit lotto. In that regard, we were similar to so many industries that revolve around ideas, research, intellectual assets, and other intangible products and services. So we had to perceive success as just putting together a great operation. If we thought we had to hit lotto every time, we'd never do anything.

The only option we ever have in counterintelligence is to buy the ticket, take the ride, roll the dice, and see what happens. That's a reasonable stance, but only if we made rational decisions and took reasonable actions.

Despite that, this would probably be the last time, for the foreseeable future, that I'd have the opportunity to buy my lotto ticket.

If I failed to recruit the general, but he stayed quiet about it, I'd probably survive the blowback. But if the general carried our incursion to the top of Russia's grievance list, my reputation—and Jack's—would take a terrible and possibly terminal hit. In counterespionage, your reputation is your brand. The same is true in most professions.

I was just hoping that the bond between the general and the American colonel superseded the demands of politics. But Russia had its own beast to feed—and, God knows, it loved trouble.

I enlisted the help of several sharp agents, and a CHS who had been working Russia with me for some time. They were all comfortable with my aggressive tempo, and we moved fast.

The more we learned about the general, the more optimistic I became. He was definitely a member of the Russian military intelligence, the GRU, but he wasn't a typical one, because he was also a gifted diplomat and general line officer.

Although movies don't portray the bureaucratic aspect of international espionage, the standard GRU officer is very similar to any big-business careerist, wherever they may be. They tend to be very risk-averse, focusing on mere survival until they reach positions so lofty that they're protected by scapegoats, money, and institutional rules. Then they become even more risk-averse, because they don't want to lose the good thing they've got.

They're also generally micromanagers, because they don't trust the people working under them to be as cautious as they are.

Another trait of me-first bureaucrats—in the government and out—is being clock-watchers who are more interested in getting through the day than in cranking out achievements.

Careerists are also savants at sucking up to people above them for protection and advancement, and being hard on people beneath them, so they can offer them up as pre-certified sacrificial lambs when the occasion demands.

They're also name-droppers, and are adept at scooping up credit and shifting blame.

They're even good at acting confident, especially when they feel insecure—which is most of the time—so they tend to adorn their offices with a Wall of Ego, comprised of photos of them with major players, and certificates of merit.

In meetings, the company guys usually remain quiet while others voice controversial ideas, but are gung-ho as soon as the boss gives the Go.

All in all, they're usually not the kind of people with whom you can develop predictable, positive relationships. These people climb with sickening regularity to the top of the pyramid, where they blight the lives of those beneath them with their insecurity, inaction, secrets, and infighting.

As our information about the general piled up, I wasn't seeing *any* of these tells.

The traits were also absent from the character of our guy, the colonel.

I could see how they might become friends.

The American colonel was a hard-core patriot, and from my multiple contacts and multiple meetings, I got the impression that he had a certain nostalgia for the bad old days of armed conflict and heroic action, and was itching to do something important—even if it carried the danger that always accompanies counterespionage activities against Russia.

The colonel's military record showed that even though he was as mission-oriented as a marine rifleman, he was also schooled in the manners of diplomacy, having spent the last years of his service as a military diplomat at a European embassy. He was there at the same time that the Russian general was working at *his* country's embassy. So they'd met at a number of international social events, and had become friendly rivals, each more vested in the achievement of personal honor and world stability than in political gain.

That quality of character is relatively common among career military people. Officers from nations all across the world gather together in these foreign posts and ride out invasions, trade wars, treaties, coalitions forming and fading, and presidents coming and going—but throughout the ebb and flow of history, they toast the same toasts, drink the same drinks, and talk the same talk, forming allegiances that often blur strict adherence to their own country's policies.

If this particular American colonel couldn't get me a meeting with the Russian general, nobody could.

After about a month of surveillance, we found out that the general would soon be soon traveling to Las Vegas with his wife on a junket that was more play than work. I wanted Vegas to be our ground zero for the meet-up.

Our narrative was that the colonel happened to be in Vegas at the same time as the Russian general: small world! But not so small that the general wouldn't suspect something. That was fine. We wanted him to think about his options before he even knew he had them, and let his optimism inflate them.

Near the end of their short mutual stay, the colonel would schedule a couple of events, like drinks in the late afternoon, then dinner with the wives. After dinner, the colonel would say that he had a friend in special services who had great access to New York's Thanksgiving Day parade. The friend—me, as you've probably guessed—had invited the colonel to come and told him to bring a couple of guests.

The general would be smart enough to decode the rest.

I took every step of the op to Jack, and to the whole team. The team was functioning flawlessly, and everybody was great. Smart questions, but not too many. Excitement. Eagerness. Total transparency about Jack's approval process.

At this stage of his career, Jack's approvals had to come from national headquarters, at the J. Edgar Hoover Building in Washington, D.C. That made things harder, because Washington has a way of turning character upside down, and making people greedy for the glamour and power of the place. But Jack never mentioned the pressure he was under, and he was oblivious to glamour.

On an almost daily basis, Jack was giving me a tell of trust—similar to the following ones—and my morale was soaring. He could see my satisfaction, and he fed off it. So did our team. I was still working closely with Jesse, along with a crew of people who were so good that I called them the Magnificent Seven. With Jack leading this operation, it felt like I was finally where I belonged.

The patterns of behavior from all the people involved were coalescing into a finely crafted mosaic.

I could smell my first lotto.

TEN POSITIVE TELLS FOR PATTERNS OF ACTIONS

1. People remain loyal to you when others are irrationally critical of you. It's easy to be loyal to people at the top of the food chain, but that's not really loyalty—it's just survival. When someone chooses to *suffer* from being on your side, you know that instinct comes from deep within, and is probably a core element of their character.

One of the best things they can offer you is an objective appraisal of why you're being unjustly criticized. A realistic fact of life is that when somebody has a problem with you, they usually have a fairly good reason. That's a hard truth, but if you accept it, you'll be astounded at how it can streamline your conflicts.

There are people in the world who are simply and solely destructive, but you probably don't work with one. Find the truth in a criticism, and you'll grow in the eyes of everyone.

This doesn't make you a pushover. It makes you somebody who's wedded to rational thought: a hallmark trait of positive, effective people.

2. When you ask someone for details or documentation about a problem, they provide it immediately. Many people stall, and try to present something that lets them off the hook. They comb their records for the documents that show them in a good light. Or they look for excuses. If there's a delay, you'll never really know.

And when you don't know, you can't predict. When you can't predict, you've got an even bigger problem.

3. When someone repeats a story about themselves or one of their actions, it never varies. But when somebody changes major components, they're probably not very honest. Law enforcement and national security officials commonly depend on this phenomenon in determining the truth.

Consistency means predictability, and predictability lies at the heart of trust.

4. People opt out of conversations when they degenerate into gossip. Helpful, dependable people don't find amusement in other people's problems.

Insecure people, on the other hand, *need* that vicarious thrill, because of their own self-doubt. They have a deep-seated fear that they are not good enough, or don't have enough, and actually enjoy hearing about the foibles of others.

The only thing that good allies want from those around them is healthy, happy relationships. It's not very titillating—but it makes friends, and makes money.

5. People are never critical about their family members, even when it would be justified. A common behavior I've never understood is how a husband (or wife—it goes either way) thinks he can build himself up by putting his wife down. All it makes me think is: *You're* the one who married her, so what does that make *you*?

Being critical is one of the cruelest ways of being judgmental, and judgmentalism is poison for a positive situation. It makes almost everybody wonder what they're being judged about, and scares them away.

If you're willing to judge your own spouse, everybody must be fair game.

6. People avoid hot-button issues, such as politics or religion, with people they don't know well. This is one manifestation of a tremendously important principle of positive behavior that I've mentioned: *seeking context.*

We all have our own complex, multifaceted context, and when someone understands it, they usually understand us. When they don't, understanding evaporates, judgment begins, and allegiance is lost.

That's why effective people tread lightly around sensitive issues when they're with someone they don't know well. Their goal is to have healthy relationships, and that starts with making people feel accepted and comfortable.

7. People display consistent personalities in their professional and personal lives. Like other self-evident truths, this one is so obvious that it often gets overlooked. In matters of core values, there can be no dichotomies. Self is self.

Consistency = Predictability = Trust = Success.

8. People sometimes cite moral or philosophical obligations, including honesty and fairness, in business situations. You can usually trust people who aren't afraid to admit that there are more important things than making money.

These people tend to be successful, partly because people trust them. Some people think that's ironic. I don't.

9. Someone's social media postings reflect the same personality that you see in their professional life. This is the e-version of personal and professional consistency. And thank God for the e-version: It's accessible, it's durable, and its ubiquitous.

Social media is the lie detector of the new millennium.

10. After you hire someone, they actually have the skills they said they did during the hiring process. Or, after you get hired, your bosses do exactly what they said they would.

Nothing is a better tell of trust than patterns of honest behavior.

No boss likes to hear: "I guess I didn't know as much about this as I thought—*but I'm a fast learner!*"

No new employee likes to hear: "We need to restructure your hours and responsibilities."

These statements are especially frustrating when they come very shortly after hiring, because it implies that somebody was lying all along. By then, it's usually too late to do anything.

Nothing is more gratifying than seeing someone do exactly what they said they would. It gives you faith in them—and faith in yourself, too, for making them an ally.

Now ask yourself: Have you recognized any of the tells of trust-based behavior among the people you work for, and those who work for you? Does one person stand out?

April 2009
Hillary's Damn Button

In hindsight, the Vegas op was too good to be true—but only by the measure of its outcome. Outcome is huge, of course. But the more I learn about human behavior, the more I see that outcomes can be measured not just by money, or hitting a political target, but also by coalescing with the right people. Putting together my team ultimately brought me far more tangible gain than hitting lotto would have. I kept most of the core players with me, and we hit some major targets that I'll tell you about later. Some of them even followed me to the Behavioral Analysis Program. There's no way I would have traded that for hitting lotto.

Here's how it went down, short version: The colonel made the parade pitch and the general said he would think about it overnight. The next day, he told the colonel that he had "seen enough parades in my life"—a response that had nothing to do with parades and everything to do with his loyalty to Russia. They shook hands and parted.

I waited several weeks for the storm to hit.

It never did. The general's loyalty to his country was apparently tempered by his loyalty to his friend, whom he did not rat out (Positive Tell #1). So I won the consolation prize. We'd run a tight op with a solid fail-safe mechanism—and in the Bureau, that's considered a successful mission.

I worked on many more operations with Jack over the next few years, then had an opportunity to move to the FBI's Norfolk Field Office, where the Chesapeake Bay hits the Atlantic. For me, it was a dream destination. My treacherous commute from the suburbs to Manhattan had been killing my family time, and I had two young children who loved living near the beach, with Dad home most of the time. I knew Jack would approve of my move, because he had kids of his own, and applied the same dedication and nurturing to them that he'd shown everyone at work (Positive Tell #7).

Despite his best efforts at home, though, Jack had pressures similar to mine, and two of his kids were acting out their frustration. One of them caused a serious problem, but Jack refused to judge his child. Instead, he got a transfer to FBI Headquarters in Washington, D.C., which was far more conducive to a good family life (Positive Tell #5).

And a few years later, he found an opening for me on his new team. I couldn't resist working at the epicenter of American law enforcement. We moved to D.C. That was when my troubles started.

I came up with a hot op. It had lotto written all over it. One of Russia's richest oligarchs, who had a line straight to Putin, was having visa problems. I wanted to help him "solve" them.

But Jack didn't seem impressed. He was clearly different in D.C.— less opinionated, more conservative, less flexible. He was still pleasant with me, but distant. We shared some very enjoyable lunches, but not much real contact. Mostly, there was way less of it. He was cocooning socially, so at least he was consistent (Positive Tell #9).

It was like night and day, and I didn't know why.

Then Secretary of State Hillary Clinton went to Russia with a gimmicky red "reset" button that symbolized State's desire for a new, improved relationship between the two countries.

That same day, Jack sent me a detailed memo explaining why my operation was contrary to the red-button détente, which he'd known about for weeks (Positive Tell #2).

I appreciated the information. But it wasn't great news for our Russia team.

I went to his office the next day, where he reiterated the whole story, exactly as he'd laid it out in the memo, clearly relieved that he no longer had to keep the secret of the red button (Positive Tell #3). He said the worst part of his new job was having to keep things confidential from virtually everyone he worked with on a daily basis, which was different from keeping secrets *within* your own team. He equated it to lying (Positive Tell #8). There was truth in that, but I assured him that I understood the necessity for secrecy.

He said that the only thing he liked about working at headquarters was that people were scrupulously careful about offending others—which some might call political correctness—and that, contrary to the movies, there was a dearth of gossip, at least in the Hoover building (Positive Tells #6 and #4).

I told him I was grateful for his honesty and that I'd been as uncomfortable with the deceitful element of the deep-dive subterfuge as he'd been (Positive Tell #10). That may sound like an odd conversation between two career spies, but in the final analysis, espionage and counterespionage in the twenty-first century is just another business. (Also there's now almost as much spycraft in private industry as there is in government.)

I realized that Jack's core values were intact, and that he hadn't really changed. He was just dealing with a new context that consisted of a much broader picture, consisting of not just the FBI, but the State Department and the White House.

Now he was protecting the people under him by protecting himself. And he was also protecting us from *ourselves,* and our sometimes dangerous dreams of glory.

Once again, I'd learned the stark limitations of judging human behavior with such binary qualities as good and bad.

It was clear, though, that after all my years of working Russia, my career had just hit a speed bump—about three feet tall. Jack mentioned that there was a major opening in the Behavioral Analysis Program.

It was for the position of director.

"Think you might be interested in that?" he asked.

DEBRIEFING

CHAPTER 6:
"DETERMINE THE DEALBREAKERS"

SIGN #4: ACTIONS

Key Quote: "For good or ill, it's your actions that define you, much more obviously and accurately than what you say or how you feel."

Key Message: To predict what someone will do, actions—past and present—must be analyzed objectively, systematically, and rationally, because people frequently change, and situations always change.

THE TAKEAWAYS

1. **Patterns:** Past patterns of honesty and fairness can sometimes crumble when people are no longer held accountable, due to power, wealth, or anonymity.
2. **Character:** Actions are the most tangible, observable, and measurable indicator of a person's character. That's primarily why action is one of the six signs for behavior prediction.
3. **Morals:** A strong moral code heightens predictability, but can change over time.

Ten Positive Tells for Patterns of Actions
1. They remain loyal while others are irrationally critical.
2. They fulfill documentation requests immediately.

3. Their versions of stories never change.

4. They don't participate in gossip.

5. They don't complain about their families.

6. They avoid divisive topics.

7. Their work personality is essentially the same as their home personality.

8. They sometimes cite moral obligations in business situations.

9. Their social media is consistent with their professional life.

10. They live up to what they said during the hiring process.

Ten Negative Tells for Patterns of Actions

1. They are not fully transparent about their past.

2. They treat powerful people better than others.

3. They have gaps or exaggerations on their résumés.

4. They regard their competitors as enemies.

5. They have a history of irregular behavior in their personal life.

6. You feel like you don't know them, even after close, prolonged contact.

7. They are tight-lipped about past colleagues.

8. They are critical about their colleagues' personal lives.

9. Their behavior is often inconsistent.

10. It's hard for them to accept responsibility.

7

LISTEN FOR THE REVEAL

Sign #5: LANGUAGE

Does this person know how to communicate in a positive way? Or do they talk trash?

September 17, 2018, 4:00 p.m.
Corporate Spooks

Our plane banked low over the San Francisco Bay, and it was so late in the day that only the triangular tip of the glassy Transamerica Pyramid was still glinting like gold in the sun. That was appropriate: I was here for money.

More specifically, I was here to find another job, because I was set to retire from the FBI in a matter of weeks. I was looking for ways to apply my expertise in intelligence to the private sector, and a few weeks earlier I'd gotten an email from a division head of a prominent corporate security firm based in S.F. He invited me to consult for a couple of days, in what appeared to be a tryout for full-time employment.

The pay would be great, but that was not what I was excited about. I'd been extremely impressed by the division head's email, because it was incredibly grounded in the principles that had guided my years of work in the Behavioral Analysis Program, and had blossomed into my system for sizing people up.

In less than 150 words, he'd touched on some of the most basic pillars of positive, sane, trustworthy behavior.

He sought my thoughts and opinions. That was the whole point of his email. In short notes, people tend to start most of their sentences with "I." His was all "you."

He validated my context. He indicated that he understood my style of operating in an industry similar to his. Understanding is a powerful quality, and is not mere flattery. Flattery tends to be broad, and is often done to manipulate, but validation is much more specific and is done to find common ground.

He spoke in terms of my priorities. He wanted to know what my top interests were, and how I might be able to benefit from his firm.

He empowered me with choice. He left the timing, the agenda, and the future of our relationship up to me.

The content was excellent, because the absolute essence of great communication is to focus on the other person, instead of yourself.

He was rational and reasonable. Those two qualities should always be synonymous—but they're not: Somebody can very rationally suggest something that's unreasonable. And that can sometimes result in the negative definition of "rationalizing"—as in "manipulating facts to support an idea." He did neither. He was straight-up facts.

Also, his *presentation of those concepts* was perfectly consistent with their content. That combination comprises what I call the language of trust.

Whenever I hear it, I feel a kindred spirit calling out to me.

This guy sounded like a dream boss.

Trusting Your Boss

Having a boss you can trust with your ideas, desires, and financial future can make almost any job great. But enduring a tyrant you don't trust and respect—and who doesn't trust and respect you—can be slow professional suicide.

For that matter, it's hard to robustly trust *anyone* who has direct power over you, because too much is at stake to be complacent about it.

We all know that supervisors have more to worry about than just *our* welfare and that their major concerns revolve around their own well-being. Besides, it's equally hard for *them* to trust *you*—a situation that's a setup for reciprocal suspicion.

If you don't trust your supervisors, your doubt can become a self-fulfilling prophecy, even if you try to hide it. Most bosses take lack of trust as an insult, and often conclude that if you're worried about them, you must have a good reason to be. Then you've got a real problem.

But when you apply a rational system to your assessment of their behaviors, you can suspend the emotionalism that clouds your perceptions—and you'll often find that you really *do* trust them.

Once you find a way to trust your managers, it puts you in a firm position to build healthy, mutually beneficial relationships with them. When that happens, you can begin to transform them from being supervisors to mentors, and eventually even peers.

As you rise, with their blessing, it's easier for you to see the broad, big-picture perspective that bosses are generally required to have. With that perspective, you won't become emotionally hijacked if your boss needs you to make a sacrifice for the benefit of your company.

Of course, in the real world, there are plenty of lousy bosses. Some of them try to limit your success on purpose, either to elevate themselves, to take credit for something you did, or to use you as a scapegoat. The typical reaction to that almost impossible situation is to rebel against it, try to escape, or just cower and do nothing. It's pure essence of fight-flight-freeze—but only if you *allow* it to be.

If, on the other hand, you can stay rational and recognize the bosses' limitations as trustworthy, generous people, you can predict these kinds of problems and not be caught off guard. You'll probably be rewarded for not overreacting, and your mature response might turn a negative into a positive.

September 17, 2018, 5:00 p.m.
Silicon Valley

I'd started the day on the East Coast by giving a presentation shortly after dawn, and I looked forward to cruising an Uber to the luxury hotel that the company had booked for me, eating a pricey (nongovernmental) room service dinner, and crashing for the night.

But when I got out of my gate, I saw a guy holding a placard with my name, and he told me the division head was waiting in a car at the curb. Felt good. The guy cared enough to drop me at the hotel personally.

He hopped out of his car to greet me, flashing a bright, dentally perfected smile, and gave me a hundred-dollar handshake: perfect firmness and timing, with the hint of a two-handed grasp. It's a minor but pleasing nonverbal, because it says somebody is at least trying. And he had a good car: a rugged, six-figure Mercedes AMG that screamed money and muscle.

He was well barbered and wearing a cashmere Armani sport coat, with jeans that probably cost about the same. In corporate intelligence, all the players wear money and drive money, because money attracts money, within the company and outside it. In the top private security corporations, you always see glitzy watches and flashy suits—it's all about the bling. But these days, you also see no tie, no jacket, six-figure sneakers, and a designer shirt with the tail out, intended to say Rich but Young.

As I settled in for the ride south to Silicon Valley, he invited me to call him not just by his first name, but by his nickname.

But for the sake of privacy protection, let's call him Mr. X—a name that reveals nothing, similar to the standard FBI code for an unnamed country, Erehwon, which is "nowhere" spelled backward.

"You haven't told me what department you manage," I said. I hadn't seen anything about him online.

He smiled warmly, seeming to luxuriate in the safety of secrecy, and then said, "Murders and Assassinations." He meant mergers and acquisitions, and narrowed his function to chief of security.

That was why he'd been so cryptic. A blockbuster global merger was unfolding, and he had either wanted me to know he was involved, or *didn't* want me to know. The companies in play were not household names, but they were both bigger than either of the companies in a recent mega-merger: Amazon and Whole Foods.

Every Fortune 500 corporation has its own team of merger analysts, who pore over the spreadsheets and databases, but even hard numbers are tough to trust at the monolithic level, due to the wizardry of corporate accountants. So the multinationals hire corporate security specialists for their M&A division, to look for the proverbial dirt under the fingernails of the company they're targeting for a takeover.

His department's job would be to pick up raw data and scraps of facts that revealed hidden weaknesses or strengths that the other company had "overlooked." But since the fine points were hidden, his tradecraft would involve cold-calling dozens of executives in a process called "elicitation": gathering and garnering information without the other person realizing that they're giving it.

The info stretched from intellectual property to less obvious elements of proprietary information, such as wages, health benefits, 401(k) funding, parking spaces—anything that contributed to the bottom line of worth and indebtedness, or that showed discrepancies in a company's bookkeeping. Very prominent people often lied. It's another example of the "power paradox" of unethical, dishonest behavior among people with limited accountability. And sometimes the companies were just running fishing operations. Chinese companies loved to feign interest in American companies, to figure out how they could undercut them. They made lowball offers and grabbed as much data as they could.

Forty of the largest countries in the world have a combined total of corporate security divisions that is larger than their nation's number of police officers. In the United States, there are about half again as many corporate security agents as police officers and sheriffs.

Worldwide, there are about twenty million corporate security officers, all governed more by the rules and cultures of their companies than by those of their countries, with incomes of about $200 billion.

So it was easy enough to understand where the nice car came from. And it was easy enough to dream about buying one myself.

I really wanted to like this guy. *Whoops!* Correction: I really wanted to *trust* this guy.

I'd learned enough about Mr. X's company to know that their division managers made all hiring decisions autonomously, that they cherry-picked the best of the best, and that their workforce tended to stay, even though they could bolt to an even bigger and richer company—like Booz Allen Hamilton, which has about twenty thousand employees, or Black Cube, a flashy international firm with roots in Israel's intelligence agency, Mossad.

Of all the nests I could possibly land in, this was probably the most well feathered. But like almost any other job, it all started with *trusting the boss*—and that was what I would investigate over the next few days. Spending just three days inside the head of a corporate intelligence officer might sound impossible, but that's the kind of thing I can do now, with my trust-evaluation system.

I didn't need to know all his secrets. I just needed to know that *what he told me was true*, especially if it had anything to do with me or my possible job. I didn't even know if Mr. X was genuinely interested in me, or was just trying to elicit information, but for the purposes of investigation, it didn't make much difference. He had his agenda and I had mine, and the goal now was to see if he and I were headed in the same direction. If we were, we'd probably want to vest in each other's success. If not, so be it.

I settled into the soft leather seat, and the ride was so smooth it felt like floating. It lulled me into the same torpor I'd felt about eighteen hours earlier, when I'd awakened before dawn on the East Coast.

I slipped into a luxurious reverie of hope and peace. For almost thirty years, I'd given everything I had to the country, and to the study of trust, and it was time to give something to myself and my family. I really didn't know what was coming. All I knew was that, one way or another, I'd learn something. I hoped it wasn't the hard way. But at this moment, life had never felt so easy.

Unleashing the Power of Language

Because the whole aim and end of language is to *tell* someone something, language itself is *one long tell*—and thereby the most transparent and easily accessible of the six signs.

Even a message that's cloaked in vagaries, corporate jargon, hidden agendas, and political correctness can be extremely revealing, if you know how to listen systematically—as do almost all investigators, including FBI agents. The system I've been showing you is as good as any that are used throughout the intelligence community.

The single most common way, and the easiest way, to sift trust from trickery is to analyze a person's spoken and written words—for vocabulary, phrasing, and delivery, as well as content.

The content of any message is the most important element, but its delivery system—its vocabulary, tone, mood, modifiers, and body language—can also be eminently telling, especially when those sometimes involuntary choices unmask feelings that aren't consistent with the content.

Nonverbal communication is a particularly important element in assessing language, mostly because of the obvious: It's another form of language. When nonverbals are interpreted accurately, they can be one of the best tells for exposing contradictions, seeing through false promises, and accurately measuring sincerity.

Assessing language accurately is generally more difficult at work than anywhere else. When you're at home or with friends, the atmosphere is much more likely to be relaxed, which makes it easier to have transparent, meaningful exchanges.

Communicating at work is complicated by the fact that almost everyone has the same direct, or indirect, goal: Making money. It's especially difficult to communicate outside your own company. In this often overheated, fast-forward arena, one of the most difficult professional tasks of all is having to cold-call people. In an era of multitasking and mega-networking, the chore of cold calling isn't just for salespeople, but for practically everyone who needs to contact strangers from other companies.

So cold calling is a great test of someone's ability to identify trustworthy people and to inspire those people to trust *them*. Those two actions often unfold simultaneously and synergistically, as relationships are made and deepened.

Often, though, the cold call lasts about a minute and creates nothing except an even greater fear of rejection.

This kills deals by the dozen and costs everybody not just lost money, but lost time and lost sleep.

Also, many people just aren't very good at communicating simply because they haven't studied it with the same intensity that they've applied to their core skills. This tends to occur less commonly among those who work at people-oriented jobs—everything from being a social worker to a salesperson—but is relatively more pronounced among people who work in science and technology.

So as we move toward an increasingly technology-dominated economy, it's important to remember that millions of people just haven't been trained in communication.

The CEO of LinkedIn, Jeff Weiner, recently noted on CBS that the greatest skill gap in American business is the seemingly simple task of communicating. That's partly because countless people are blind to the effects of their words, don't know how to listen, and preen and preach as if the world revolves around them.

That perception is often understandable, because their *own* world *does* revolve around them. Just not yours. That's the part they don't get.

People like that, though, aren't the scary ones, because their communicative behavior is so bad that it's easy to see. The scary ones are the master manipulators who talk the talk but stab the back.

September 17, 2018, 6:45 p.m.
The Silicon Weeds

"Robin!" said Mr. X.

Half asleep from a long day of travel and the luxury of floating silently down the freeway, I was startled but tried not to show it. I had a strong feeling that Mr. X wasn't very fatigue-friendly. He'd been rattling off a series of business theories he'd read about that were hard to follow, and I was impressed. I'd never met someone with quite his mastery of books and business before. But he was going too fast for me to feel informed, and I thought that might have been his intention. You never know until somebody starts talking. Speaking is much more revealing than emails, because emails are naturally truncated, and can also be edited. That's partly why they're so popular.

It's also why text messages, even more than emails, can be so dangerous. Contrary to conventional culture, I think some things are *too* quick and convenient.

"You know Joe Navarro and Chris Voss, right?" he said, and I nodded. I'd worked with both of them in the Bureau, and now they had successful careers as consultants and authors. "They came out here," he said. But that was all. I assumed he was either trying to make me feel comfortable by mentioning mutual friends—or *not* comfortable, by mentioning possible competitors for the job he had in mind for me: whatever *that* was. All I knew was that I'd been offered a two-day consultancy, and even that was mostly a mystery.

I always try to keep an open mind about what people say, and I listen hard. Often as not, I can tell if I can trust them in a matter of minutes. But Mr. X was relatively hard to read, a common quality in Fortune 500 management—and a virtual epidemic in the F500 *intelligence* sector.

Then he mentioned another acquaintance and said, "Good guy, but slow on the uptake." I agreed with the opinion, but responded neutrally. The guy he mentioned had a problem, but it was none of my business.

"You don't agree?" he prodded. It really wasn't a question, so I just smiled. Smiling solves a shocking number of problems. "Got it," he said, and I smiled again.

"Do me a favor," he said, "and see how our stock did today." I checked it with my phone and told him his company was up six points. "Awesome!" he said. "That's two months' pay!" And that was the end of that. Either he was trying to show me how much money he was making, or he was just happy. It was another one of those bifurcated paths of communication that only get sorted out as the words pile up and the data builds.

"Do you know why you're here?" he asked abruptly. I just shrugged. "To teach my people about trust. That's your genius."

Then he was off to the races again about business, probing my background and knowledge on everything from elicitation, to rapport building, to trust, to influence: the various areas in which I've worked most often. He was seeking my ideas and opinions, as he had in that first introductory email, but this time it was all about what *I* could do for *him*.

But that's common, so I didn't let it bother me. Studies conducted as early as a hundred years ago had already started showing that about 40 to 50 percent of everything we say is about ourselves. For some reason, it seemed to me as if people would have been less self-absorbed in that simpler era, but I guess it's just endemic to human behavior.

In one of the more recent behavioral studies I read, researchers saw that when people talked about themselves to somebody, the pleasure centers in their brains lit up, powered by happy hormones like dopamine, serotonin, and even the post-orgasm and bonding hormone oxytocin. Most of the people did it even after researchers offered to pay them to talk about the other person. When they did let the other person talk, that person's brain went straight to its happy place, too.

I've also learned that men are even bigger conversation hogs than women, and focus mostly on self-aggrandizement. Women talk more about bonding and networking, but still mostly in relation to themselves.

It's been shown that the people in a group who speak the most concisely tend to be the ones who are considered the most trustworthy and wise. It's because they look as if they don't feel the need to *sell* their ideas, which makes the listeners *more* likely to buy in.

The concept of *evoking* a feeling in someone, rather than just *showing* it to them, is invoked in the acting profession as: "Let the audience do the acting." Corollaries include: "Let the buyer do the selling," and "Let the reader do the writing."

I got the feeling that Mr. X didn't even feel very comfortable with what *he* was saying, because I was getting too many nonverbals that were inconsistent with the points he was making. I especially noticed a strange nervous tic that made him shake his head—in *dissent* with his words—when he should have been nodding.

He kept asking questions—which typically indicates somebody's interest in the other person's opinion. But when I told him how I felt about things, he'd usually contradict me. It seemed reflexive, as if he would have disagreed with *whatever* I would've said. Maybe it was his way of trying to control.

We pulled up in front of a twenty-story building near Palo Alto. "Let's go see the Eskimos!" he said.

"Eskimos?"

"My guys. I call 'em Eskimos because all they do is make cold calls. To find stuff out about the companies we're researching. Your job is to teach them how to be trusted in fifteen minutes!"

"Why fifteen?"

"Because if you cold-call executives who are smart enough to know what we need to know, all they'll *give* you is fifteen minutes. On a *good* day."

Apparently we weren't at the hotel. It was his company's building, and it looked as if my workday was just starting. I'd only billed him for two days, since it's customary to have travel-days off, but now it looked as if he wanted an extra half-day. *Damn.* I was tired. But at least I'd learned that he liked to get more than he'd bargained for. That was good to know. I felt like yawning, but didn't let myself.

1. People don't jump to conclusions. They jump to *facts,* asking enough questions to fully understand you before they make any comments of their own. Jumping to conclusions is a terribly common trait that tends to cause more conflicts than the issues that are supposedly the *sources* of conflict.

The trait comes straight from fear, and usually leads to even more fear—and fewer friendly contacts. It also creates emotional hijacking.

There's a reason why one of the most common synonyms for a fight, an argument, or another from of discord is called a "misunderstanding."

2. People make you feel good when they talk. That's because they know the single most potent key to being liked: It's not how you make people feel about you. It's how you make them feel about *themselves.*

When somebody makes you feel intelligent, understood, important, or powerful, in a sincere way, how could you possibly not like them?

When somebody tells you that *they* are intelligent, understanding, important, and powerful, how could you possibly stand one more minute of their company?

This is one of the rare ideas that can change your life, or at least the way you talk to people.

3. People talk more about your similarities than your differences. They understand that most people, day to day, generally agree about most things. How could we not? We all have the same basic needs and the same basic rights. We all want to be perceived as good people and to behave as good people. We all suffer, we all feel joy, we all win, and we all lose.

When you're *looking* for differences, you will find them. The easiest way is to presume that someone disagrees with you. Another way is to *ask* them if they disagree with you. Why bother?

Every time you do that, you take a significant risk of making your negative assumptions come true.

Start with your agreements, and meander to the *disagreements*, if you must. Unity and agreement lie in the hearts of all humans. Discord lies at the margins, and every time you fixate on it, you marginalize yourself.

4. People look at you closely when you talk. They don't stare off into space, glance at their phone, peek at the TV, or look straight ahead.

Why? They're looking for how you *feel* about what you're saying. Your words alone rarely tell the whole story, and even if they do, people still feel ignored when you don't look at them.

The people you like to talk to keep their eyes as open as their ears.

5. People don't speak like the talking heads on TV. In this age of splintered media, TV newspeople tell the audience what they know they want to hear and—guess what?—the audience thinks they're brilliant.

They don't present facts. Just arguments. They don't talk. They accuse and pose.

It's considered "lively." It's deadly.

In entertainment, drama is an art. In communication, it's a vice.

6. They almost never win arguments. (Have you already stopped reading? Don't worry—there's a happy ending.) By the time a discussion has degenerated from talking to arguing, and then reaches the stage of either winning or losing, you've both lost.

Have you ever "won" an argument in which you were positive that the "loser" wasn't resentful, vengeful, offended, or otherwise alienated?

People never really win until they stop fighting. That's not a Zen philosophy. That's the way life goes.

Any way you look at it, there's more to winning than just getting your way on a particular day.

Here's the happy ending: By the time you've lost enough to never want to fight again—but just talk—you can't do anything *but* win. It happens all the time, and makes people wonder why they ever wasted so much time trying to make someone else lose.

7. People are easy to understand. That doesn't mean it's easy for them. Being clear is hard work.

The hard part is having good ideas, because clarity lays bare the ideas it conveys. Complexity conceals and simplicity reveals.

Shoot for deep and simple, not shallow and complicated.

8. The moral content of their speech goes beyond political correctness. They're far more concerned about being *morally* correct.

When you have a big heart and a clear conscience, you don't feel obligated to advertise how magnanimous and hip you are.

With the decline of organized religion, political correctness took its place. But it's mostly composed of good manners, rather than sacrifice from helping the less fortunate.

I love good manners, but they don't constitute a complete and robust moral code. PC is not a religion. It's just being polite.

9. People talk about you more than themselves. That's somewhat similar to Positive Tell #2 (the importance of making people feel good about themselves), but it has a different goal: inspiring you to vest in someone else's success, and vice versa.

If someone encourages you to be the center of attention, it's often because they're trying to see if you have similar goals. If you do, they'll probably want to do things with you. Because the majority of people talk mostly about themselves. So this is a relatively rare trait, but one of the best possible tells of exemplary behavior.

10. People talk the same to rich and poor alike. To them, all people deserve equal respect. Almost all people believe that they are fair and kind to almost everybody, but it's often a delusion. It's extremely difficult to treat all people the same, and most of us sometimes stray from that ideal.

You can't trust people who are egotistical, condescending, and discriminatory—even if they don't treat *you* that way.

September 17, 2018, 7:00 p.m.
Life Among the Eskimos

After Mr. X and I arrived at his company, I shook off my fatigue, grabbed some coffee in the building's lobby, and followed him to his division's floor. I was expecting a crowd, but discovered that his whole division was fewer than ten people. Security teams like privacy, but even by that profession's standards, having a whole floor for a handful of people was an impressive indication of this team's value to its company.

Mr. X brought his entire team to the center of the floor, which felt as big as a parking lot, because some of the inner walls had been reduced to just load-bearing posts, creating a very rare 360-degree panorama. Every window held a view of what is arguably the world's most powerful small town.

Most of the staff was clustered near the middle, in individualized, multimodal workstations. It was a very nouveau, Google-like formation that was apparently intended to reflect democracy. (As long as everybody knows who the *boss* is—that kind of democracy . . .)

With his endemic sense of showmanship, Mr. X pushed a button that revealed a virtually endless bank of cabinets holding vast rows of thin bound booklets, all in the red-brown color of dried blood. Even though I lived in the epicenter of the world's largest bureaucracy, I'd never seen so much . . . *paper.* I felt like I was looking at an endangered species.

"What is *this?*" I asked, genuinely shocked.

"Our *scripts,*" Mr. X said proudly. I didn't know what he meant. "For the *calls!* The *cold* calls!"

He handed me one, and I got as far as:

GOOD _____ (MORNING, AFTERNOON), _____
(MR./MS.) _____! I'M _____, AND I REALLY APPRECIATE
YOUR TIME. HOW ARE *YOU* DOING TODAY?

"Um, professionals don't *script,*" I blurted. I had visions of somebody trying to sell me a time-share over the phone. "*Amateurs* script." I wished almost immediately that I hadn't said that. It wasn't remotely diplomatic. But it was true.

As the people closest to me studied the floor, Mr. X said, "Tell that to *Wired!*"

"Okay." I shrugged. I had no idea what he was referencing, but I'd dug myself in deep enough.

Some of the staffers glanced up with what seemed to be carefully guarded expressions of appreciation.

"How many of these are there?" I asked.

"Three thousand," Mr. X said.

Then he asked somebody to get take-out dinners at a nearby upscale restaurant. Nobody seemed surprised when he did that, so there was apparently no such thing as overtime here: just nonstop work, until the boss got tired.

He grabbed an armload of booklets, summoned me to a workstation, and handed me a red pencil. I hadn't seen a red pencil in years. "Go nuts!" he said. "And bring these up to *your* standards."

Sounded good. No matter how manipulative these crafted dialogues were, I thought I could fix them. The basic function was just to reverse the perspective and make them about the opinions, ideas, and goals of the *person being called,* instead of the caller.

You've probably already seen enough examples in this book to do the job yourself.

Fueled by caffeine from their ultragourmet coffee and snack station, I was able to plow through ten of them before dinner arrived, because the changes were relatively uniform.

To me, that's the most beautiful aspect of building trust-based relationships, even during a quick phone call. You don't need to reinvent communication; you just need to put the other person in the driver's seat.

When people first hear that, they usually think they'll lose control. But control is an illusion. *Nobody* wants to be controlled, and the moment you start trying to do it, people start resisting. Most people are even uneasy with trying to be influenced.

Genuine, lasting power—which in the final analysis is *leadership*—resides in those who become resources for the success and inspiration of others. If you can figure out where someone wants to go, and point them in that general direction, your influence can be not only profound, but appreciated. And the appreciation quickly becomes the primary source of your power.

I'll say this about Mr. X's operation, though: Dinner was amazing. Five stars. In my own plush workstation, I felt like the president of the United States enjoying the creative genius of the White House chef as I toiled into the evening.

People were really nice to me, and that renewed my confidence in Mr. X, because you can often assess the quality of executives by the caliber of the people they place around themselves.

I started giving people the finished edits of the booklets, and the delivery accelerated as I figured out the most consistent elements that needed to be fixed, and built a system to fix them. A lot of it was just changing "I" to "you" and putting a question mark at the end. It really is that simple.

As occasionally happens when exhaustion and output simultaneously peak, I reached a state of endorphin euphoria that made me think I could revolutionize corporate America's communication style. A few minutes later, I came to my senses and hit a wall. I dragged my ass into Mr. X's workspace, which was shaped like a cockpit.

"Dude," I said, "I'm fried."

He reacted as if I'd said that I'd had a minor stroke, and in a matter of minutes he'd arranged a high-speed retreat to my hotel suite, where he assured me my luggage was waiting, along with a nice dessert, a nightcap, and a wake-up call courteously structured to my own time zone. He also called me the "Cold-Call King"—CCK—and the staff picked up on it, as they gathered to say good-bye. Great people.

It was flattering. I liked Mr. X. He was a good guy—and at this late hour, liking was enough.

On my way out, he assured me that even just the changes I'd engineered already would enable his people to "win trust" in the requisite fifteen minutes. I didn't mention it, but "win trust" is a phrase I never use, because trust isn't a game, and "winning" trust makes no more sense than "winning" love. In either case, it's given freely, or it doesn't exist. Over the years, I'd tried to win both, and it had given me nothing but heartache.

TEN NEGATIVE TELLS FOR THE LANGUAGE OF TRUST

1. People think they can brag artfully. Some people wait for the right moment in a conversation to casually toss in their moment of self-promotion as mere information, or as a pertinent example, or a flash of amusing recollection.

When you give them the kudos they're looking for, they brush it off.

They also sometimes reassure you that you will be able to do something even better than they did—in the guise of encouragement—when their primary goal is to help you remember how great they are, as you struggle to do it.

If they name-drop, they mention the Big Name in a cluster of unknowns, as if they're not even aware of their status seeking.

2. People try to please you by judging people you both know. They imply that you are better than those people, or they wouldn't be confiding their disapproval.

They give you opportunities to jump in with your own disapproval of those people, as if it's a healthy form of bonding.

Meanwhile, all you're thinking is: *What do they say about* me, *when I'm not present?*

3. People are defensive. Dangerous trait! And one of the most common.

Many people feel that if they deny something, it ceases to exist.

They turn criticisms of themselves into a joke or into an offensive statement that makes no sense.

They pout. They act passive-aggressive.

They change the subject. They distort the "accusation."

Or they just withdraw.

These are the ways they put up their shields. Shields up, information out. Shields down, information in.

4. People debate. I've mentioned this previously, because it's a major problem. I'm not talking about an exchange of rational ideas. I'm talking about the hyperemotional dogfights that now dominate opposing discussions everywhere from *The Real Housewives of New Jersey* to political debates.

Debating tactics are just a string of tricks that can be shockingly effective in manipulating people.

Some of the worst include: attacking people instead of their ideas, using insinuation and innuendo, playing on fears, being sarcastic and dismissive, scapegoating, changing the subject, exaggerating or diminishing realities, putting words into people's mouths, and labeling people.

Once upon a time, you couldn't get a passing grade in English if you communicated like that. Now you can run for high public office.

5. People often speak in absolutes, such as "always" or "never." This is another form of miscommunication that causes many different problems. Absolutes are meant to support a point of view, but they're rarely true and can easily incite denial and opposition.

When somebody says, "You never compliment me," they're just begging you to say: "That's ridiculous! I remember giving you compliments!"

Even when you know that somebody is just exaggerating, it can be hard to tell if *they* know it. When absolutes go unchallenged, they have a perverse tendency to be reborn as the truth.

When you're looking for someone to trust, listen for their use of words that soften absolutes, such as "usually," "often," "probably," "practically," "sometimes," "frequently," or "generally." You may have noticed that this book is full of them. They have an almost magical ability to prevent petty bickering.

6. People tell you not to mind before they kick your teeth in. As in: "Don't take this personally, but you suck." Or: "I don't mean to be critical—*at all*—but, as I previously mentioned, you *suck*."

I could go on, but you've heard it all before.

In behavioral analysis, this is called "negating the frame," and it's one of those ugly tricks of language that do, on occasion, seem to work, by softening a blow. More often, they merely announce it.

7. People talk too much and say too little. It's usually because they're trying to hide something, or just don't have anything to say. So they try to substitute quantity for quality, especially by dropping business buzzwords, like "negative growth," "thought leader," or a currently ubiquitous cliché du jour: "strategic planning"—as if a regular plan is just a wish list.

In contrast, Winston Churchill—a gifted speaker, inspiring wartime prime minister, and Nobel laureate in literature—once wrote in *The Economist*, "Short words are best, and old words, when short, are best of all." A similar sentiment was echoed by business communications specialist L. J. Brockman, creator of the C2M2 formula, which designates the four primary characteristics of successful communications: clear, concise, memorable, and motivational.

Despite the accessibility of straight talk, brevity, and good manners, many people are afraid that if they don't dominate the conversation or shoot down the ideas of others, they'll lose control of the situation.

8. A person's body betrays them. Nonverbal communication is often a dead giveaway, and I believe that a person's face tells the most. Here are some signs of stress displayed by people who are uncomfortable with what they're saying. When you see these signs, it's wise—and often kind—to give people special attention about *why* they feel uncomfortable.

Their smile: Unlike in a genuine smile, the corners of their mouth don't go up, but are pulled straight back. The smile doesn't include their whole face. Their brows are often furrowed.

Their head angle: Their head is tilted slightly backward, rather than off to either side, and they literally look down their nose at you.

Their eyes: Unlike the wide-open eyes of someone you can trust, their eyes are somewhat lidded, and tend to be locked on you, without much movement.

These expressions are most revealing if they happen relatively often, but not all the time. The times when they're not happening provide you with a baseline for evaluation. Then, when you see these signs, you have good reason to analyze them for other tells that show how they really feel.

9. People don't know how to apologize. Apologizing is pretty easy. You say, "I'm sorry," and that's it. But that doesn't happen as often as it should, does it?

Far too commonly, people say, "I'm sorry. *But...*" Then comes the about-face, usually fueled by an accusation. *"But* I only did it because *you* did, blah, blah, blah."

This happens out of fear—particularly in fear's common disguises of arrogance, perfectionism, or some other form of superiority.

The person's central, self-dooming premise is: *It's all about me— and if I just plead not guilty to every charge, it'll stay that way.*

Quit while you're ahead.

10. People assign psychological diagnoses to themselves, as if that justifies their troubled behavior. The most common traits that are cited are depression, anxiety, and post-traumatic stress syndrome, all of which are perfectly valid for millions of people. But even though they may explain unpleasant behavior, they don't justify it.

If an overly self-conscious or unhappy person can't accept the idea that many other people suffer similarly—without inflicting their suffering on others—it will be even harder for them to get the help they desire.

September 20, 2018
Mr. X Misdirects Me

On my last day in Palo Alto—another travel day that had been shoehorned into a day's work—I talked to as many of the Eskimos as possible, getting a feel for their internal levels of comfort and satisfaction. They were all loyal to the boss, but I thought that might have reflected *their* high level of character and ethics more than his.

One of the most forthright people I met wasn't one of the Eskimos, but a man who worked in the Spies and Lies section. It was a microniche that apparently had something to do with a huge bank of databases and the creation of "pretext"—the spook-speak word for misrepresenting the actual purpose of a phone call—or some other form of penetrating an organization.

He said he'd heard that I was the Fifteen-Minute Man—the guy who could create trust in a fifteen-minute call—but that Mr. X might be misdirecting me about the bottom-line specifics of what he wanted from me.

"He tends to prevent people from seeing the big picture," the Spies and Lies guy said. "I think he's most comfortable when he's the only person who knows what's going on. Makes him feel safer, I guess."

Safer from what, I never found out, although I suspected he meant safer from an outraged multinational company, or safer from being replaced. In any case, the subject wasn't much of a conversation starter. Mystery rarely is. I didn't probe any further, since I was trying to keep a low profile at this point. But I certainly took note.

I was beginning to enjoy the exotic atmosphere, and there was a lot about Mr. X to like and admire—which created at least the verisimilitude of trust, comfort, and admiration, if not the real thing. He'd dropped all the buzzwords and business lingo (Positive Tell #7), was careful to talk about our similarities (Positive Tell #3), and paid close attention when I was talking (Positive Tell #4). He'd backed off on being argumentative (Positive Tells #6 and #1), and talked more about me than himself (Positive Tell #9). That's a lot. In any number of situations, it would be more than enough.

But I wasn't in love with the scripting process, and hadn't made a dent in his infatuation with it. He tried to flatter me by saying his Eskimos just weren't at my level—so they needed the scripts—but I was afraid he was just deceiving himself. He was good at the creation of compelling narratives, even if they were deceptive—and I don't mean that as a gratuitous criticism, because counterespionage is all about narratives and deception.

Even so, he was one of the very best wordsmiths I've ever met, but he tended to let his beautifully expressed words determine his thoughts, instead of letting his thoughts determine his words.

That trait is not uncommon among top salespeople, politicians, writers, inspirational speakers, and other professionals who are simply more fluent than thoughtful.

From my perspective, though, he seemed to be scripting manipulation. I asked him that—politely but point-blank—but he was emotionally defensive about it (Negative Tell #3).

Instead of defending his position with logic, he used another of his debating tactics, as he had when I'd first mentioned that scripting was amateurish. At that time, he'd created a false choice: If I didn't agree with him, I was disagreeing with the editors at *Wired* (Negative Tell #4).

As I was gathering my stuff to head to the airport, I remembered other red flags I'd noticed in his language. Right off the bat, he'd bragged about his stock holdings in a very indirect way, by equating them to his income (Negative Tell #1). He'd also criticized a guy we both knew, for no reason other than to intimate that he and I were better than the guy (Negative Tell #2). Also on that first day, before we even got out of the car, I'd seen him contradict himself nonverbally, by shaking his head when he should have been nodding (Negative Tell #8). That was creepy, because it seemed to reflect a deep inner conflict— a behavior problem particularly well reflected by nonverbals.

He'd also used far too many absolutes (Negative Tell #5), which can be harmless, but can also indicate an attachment to polar opposites that can metastasize into oppositional behavior: disagreeing for the sake of disagreement. Like so many other people who are argumentative, I thought that he liked to argue because he liked to win, and had no sense of my belief that by the time you're arguing, *nobody* wins.

I was also concerned about a time when he'd contradicted me. I'm fine with differing opinions, but he'd said, "I'm not implying that you know *nothing* about surveillance, but . . ." (Negative Tells #5 and #6).

He was kind enough to drive me back to the airport, and was in good spirits.

"We got a *ton* done," he said, "and I'm gonna have you *back*!"

Then he asked me if I'd like to be put on retainer. I didn't know what kind of money he had in mind, and I didn't really want to know. It would have made it harder for me to do what I'd already decided to do.

"One thing, though," he said. "We're going to take this one step further. Really *streamline* it. I'm talking about"—he paused for effect—"*thirty seconds!*"

So that was probably the misdirection that the guy from Spies and Lies had alluded to.

Mr. X, staring straight ahead—as if he was so sure about my reaction that he didn't need to look at me—said, "I'll be honest. That's what I always wanted. But I didn't know if you could wrap your head around it."

That was it. I was done. Too many surprises. Not enough predictability.

I told him so, and he practically began to cry. It was very strange. I could *never* have predicted that. But it reassured me that I'd made the right decision.

The rest of the ride was awkward. For him. I felt fine.

I was going home.

DEBRIEFING

CHAPTER 7:
"LISTEN FOR THE REVEAL"

———

SIGN #5: LANGUAGE

Key Quote: "Because the whole aim and end of language is to *tell* someone something, language itself is *one long tell*—and thereby the most transparent and easily accessible of the six signs."

Key Message: The basic content of the language of trust consists of verbal and nonverbal statements that reflect nonjudgmental, validating thoughts intended to empower others with choice. It reflects a willingness to be a resource for the benefit of others, and the willingness to vest in their success.

THE TAKEAWAYS

1. **Listen carefully:** The language of trust focuses more on the listener than the speaker, and reflects a continuous effort to understand what people want, and how to be a resource for those desires.
2. **Pay attention to nonverbal communication:** Nonverbal communication is more important and revealing for the language of trust than it is for any of the other signs, simply because it is another form of language.
3. **Avoid misunderstandings:** Lack of understanding causes so many conflicts that one of the most common synonyms for a disagreement is a "misunderstanding." Get the facts. Then talk.

Ten Positive Tells for the Language of Trust

1. They don't jump to conclusions.
2. They make you feel good when they talk.
3. They talk more about your similarities than your differences.
4. They look at you closely when you talk.
5. They don't speak like the talking heads on TV.
6. They almost never "win" arguments.
7. They're easy to understand.
8. The moral content of their speech goes beyond political correctness.
9. They talk more about you than about themselves.
10. They talk the same to rich and poor.

Ten Negative Tells for the Language of Trust

1. They use subtle forms of self-aggrandizement.
2. They try to please you by judging people you both know.
3. They're defensive.
4. They debate.
5. They often speak in absolutes, such as "always" or "never."
6. They tell you not to mind before they kick your teeth in.
7. They talk too much and say too little.
8. Their bodies betray their words.
9. They don't know how to apologize.
10. They use psychological labels to avoid accountability.

8

SEE INSIDE PEOPLE

Sign #6: STABILITY

*Does this person consistently demonstrate
emotional maturity, self-awareness, and social skills?*

Quantico, 2019
Building Your Own World

We all live in a world that is disproportionately dominated by those who are the most domineering. Our acts are often compelled by the most compulsive, and controlled by the most controlling.

Even our day-to-day moods are routinely usurped by the moody people around us, and many of our anxieties are created by the overly anxious.

These intrusive, emotionally unstable people often gain great power—not just in companies, cities, or social groups, but even in entire nations, where they callously degrade and destroy the lives of millions of people they've never met. Consider the criminal insanity of Adolf Hitler. Or Joseph Stalin. Osama bin Laden. Saddam Hussein. Pol Pot. Bashar al-Assad. These are only a few of recent history's major-league villains, and there are also millions of minor-league monsters in the world, as well as a virtually infinite number of ordinary idiots who've never learned how to act like decent human beings.

That's not how most of us would like life to be, but it's the way it's always been. The tyranny of the troubled is a sad fact of human nature that's almost as immutable as the laws of physics.

Even so, the power of the imbalanced remains reasonably bearable—unless we're called to war, taken to prison, or similarly harmed—because it's the only real price we have to pay for enjoying *our own unsung luxury of emotional stability,* while the fretful crazies stew about the problems that they've created for themselves.

The price we pay is usually worth it. To be in the mind of any of these people would be like living in hell.

Many of the most distressed and demented people—even those whose power is tiny and mundane—see themselves as superheroes, power players, or victims who now deserve to be victimizers. But that's not how other people see them. With certain exceptions, we see emotionally unstable people—no matter their place in the human hierarchy—as shaky, sly, and at least slightly deranged. Even if they're wealthy and powerful, they look like imposters to us and are impossible to respect, predict, or ally with.

You probably realized long ago, after meeting hundreds of ten-cent villains, that they acted that way because, at some point, they were so miserable that they traded their own sense of self for a reward they may already have lost, or to escape a punishment they may have deserved. But whether they won or lost the tangible prizes of life, they almost certainly lost control of their *own* lives, and that's a loss that few souls survive.

Countless troubled but courageous people—thank God—have clawed their way back from the abyss of emotional instability, but some people just can't. They lose control of their behavior and environments and become the architects of their own doom. As their desperation for control deepens, their sense of worth disintegrates, and they begin an eternal search outside themselves for the peace of mind that's only available within.

But you do not have to live in their world.

With work, luck, help—and a free country—you can create a world of your own. Not everyone will choose to live in your world, of course. That would be too much to hope for (and too much trouble!). But you can *exclude* virtually anyone you want from your world, if you're willing to move forward without them. And from that point on, no one can tell you what to do, without your consent.

That might sound risky or overly ambitious, but it's the deal that's now on the table in front of you. It's been there most of your life and it will never go away—even if you don't take advantage of it.

It's a good deal! It's the same one I made with myself years ago. And now I wake up every morning in what feels very much like my own world, tailored to fit my own desires, abilities, obligations, and goals. It's not a perfect world. (How *could* it be? *I'm* in it.) But it makes life inordinately richer in one central way: It allows me to *be myself.*

That's huge, because if you're *not* yourself, it's almost as if you don't exist. I'm sure you've met many people who have surrendered their sense of self—and that you've seen the blank look in their eyes, and heard the hollow sound of their voice.

Life can be a tough challenge for anybody, and it's easy to lose your sense of self. It happens—to at least a moderate degree, and for a finite period of time—to most people. It happened to me.

In my younger years, I was a typical type-A, all-American dumb-ass who wasn't remotely as confident as I acted, so I set out to reinvent myself, sort of like The Great Gatsby did—but I was more like The Pretty Good Gatsby.

I was luckier than most. I failed at an early age. I had the misfortune to succeed as a student and athlete in high school, and that success, and the rewards it left, revealed my emptiness. I was considered cool—but only by people *other* than myself.

Like so many people, I was my own best enemy, because I always knew which of my buttons to push, which of my fears to exaggerate, and how to piss people off if they slighted me. And the more I criticized myself, the more I rebelled against it, and hid behind my pride. With my insecurity churning, I skewed more toward arrogance than humility, believing that the only reason most people were humble was because they had a lot to be humble about. But even then, I knew my facade was paper thin.

As an antidote, and a matter of patriotism, I entered the U.S. Marine Corps with the lofty goal of shedding that callow feeling of vulnerability, longing, and unworthiness that's often called innocence. Similarly to many young people, I was filled with worry about my failings thus far, and what they might mean to my future. Those feelings emerged mostly as disappointment in myself, and as shame: just garden-variety guilt.

No matter how hard I tried, I couldn't stop feeling guilty about what I'd already done wrong, and I didn't even know what it *was*. That's youth, right?

But as I kept studying human behavior, I found that the most accurate and granular definition of guilt is: *fear of not being loved.* We're afraid that when people—or deities—discover the bad things we've done, their love for us will fade. That simple but profound threat is usually the root cause of the empty, sick feeling that always goes with guilt.

We're less likely, though, to feel remorse or shame when we think that we'll get away with something. That phenomenon is a form of the previously mentioned power paradox: Powerful people are more likely than vulnerable people to break rules, betray trust, and not worry too much about it.

But even if you're one of the rich, famous (and unindicted) people, there's still no easy way out of this dilemma, because if you hide your transgressions, you'll always know that the people who love you don't love the *real* you.

So innocence and guilt—generally seen as opposites—share some of the same shaky ground in the eternal search for love. And both can hurt.

The pain comes from facing your hunger for love, and accepting the changes in yourself that love requires, without losing your sacred sense of self. It's a balancing act, and when you attempt it, you will at some point fall.

We will all fall.

We all know that the concept of a perfect world—even one you craft around yourself—is an illusion. But it's a hard illusion to resist, and impossible to leave behind without some regret.

We all want to strip away life's illusions, but—as I learned on 9/11—who among us wants to be disillusioned? I'd lost enough of my own illusions—on that grave day—to clearly see my vast number of humbling limitations. And it actually made me feel better! That may sound paradoxical, but it's not. Most people who don't see their limitations are also largely unaware of their powers, because the nature of insight is to see everything . . . or nothing. You can't cherry-pick self-awareness.

People who can't handle the challenge of seeing inside themselves tend to preen, pose, dominate, and manipulate, never knowing that these sad acts carry them further and further from the primal desire they wanted in the first place: self-acceptance. It's the foundation of all emotional stability.

Some people who aren't emotionally stable try to compensate by being perfect—but perfectionism is generally just another face of fear. Perfectionists always want more-more-more, but people who are humble usually believe they've got nothing to prove. They think that they've already done enough to earn the right to live in their own world, without sacrificing their individuality, strengths, and desires.

So humility offers an enormous head start on the road to emotional stability. Even so, humility is one of those funny things that we all want, but don't always like. When you first sample it, you feel let down, as if you're just like everybody else. You forget that *that's what you wanted all along:* a sense of belonging, with the warmth of family, friends, and professional allies—even if every one of them has some flaws.

But if you're lucky, you meet somebody else who's humble. You accept and respect them—but not because you think they're better than you. To you, they're just another member of the tribe.

Then you see them do something incredible, and the single best and hardest lesson of emotional stability starts to sink in: *You don't have to be better than other people to be amazing.*

Here's a fact of life: No matter how hard you try, you'll never be majestically, inordinately better than you've always been—but that's good *enough*. You won't be loved by everyone, but you'll be loved *truly* by the people who are capable of true love. They'll be the only ones whose love really matters to you, because they'll love you for being you, and won't need you to fulfill the fantasies that are so important to people who are incapable of true love.

I first found that lofty level of love and acceptance in my wife and kids. Family is where most people find stability. And then it filters out to some close friends. Sadly, that's often where it ends. When many people head for work, it's often gone, because they believe in (and thereby help to create) a work-world dominated by attitudes of dog-eat-dog, killer-instincts, take-no-prisoners, nose-to-the-grindstone, trust-no-one—and all the other clichés that *just aren't necessary* in an emotionally stable, self-created world. Even the rough-and-tumble world of the Marine Corps, I found, was governed far more by camaraderie and shared mission than by aggression and selfish ambition.

After the Corps had kicked some sense into me, I gravitated naturally to the FBI, as do many people from the military who are looking for another role that will require great discipline, a way to bring their patriotism home, and the chance to serve greater gods than money and power.

By that time, I was a fairly humble, stable guy (by the crazy standards of young American males), and I believed I could be a great FBI agent during the day—and a human being at night! (My wife more or less insisted on it.)

So even as a young agent, I was still a little rough around the edges. That's me.

But it was all working!

Until September 11, 2001. All hell broke loose—even in *my world*—and peace in America never really returned.

At that time, as I've mentioned, I was working Russia, mostly in New York. I spent my days helling around Manhattan like a batshit-crazy bloodhound, sniffing out spies, and finding spies of my own. But when the Bureau was blindsided by 9/11—as was practically every three-letter agency—it gave the Russians a window of opportunity to grab back some of their empire. They invaded Chechnya and killed about fifty thousand people, mostly civilians. They unleashed a vicious storm of terror, kidnapping, hostage taking, torture of entire families, beheading, degradation, and rape, with a special focus on sex crimes, which horrified the conservative Chechen culture.

America, though, was understandably obsessed with the Middle East, and was vulnerable to Russia's propaganda programs. Their line was: "Chechnya is full of Muslim terrorists, and we're doing your dirty work *for* you—so, *you're welcome!*"

America's perception of the Russian narratives tilted toward acceptance. It was a crazy perception, and allowed the rebirth of Russia as an unstable, loose cannon nation.

The shift in attitude was alarming. I'd already learned that most aberrant behavior starts with misperception—rather than evil, or outright insanity—and that America was *choosing* to perceive Russia as benign.

I was bewildered by it—until I joined the Behavioral Analysis Program—because the BAP specialized in *why* things were happening, rather than the issues of who, what, when, or where. When the BAP taught me not to look at things from strictly my *own* context, I realized that American citizens were tolerating Russia's cruelty and greed simply because we could not, at that time, tolerate having another enemy. From the American public's context of fighting virtually permanent wars in Afghanistan and Iraq, *any* war seemed destined for disaster.

In the Behavioral Analysis Program, my understanding of human nature grew exponentially, partly because I had to parse my *own* perceptions practically every day, in order to understand those of others. It opened my eyes, and revealed a more rational, warmhearted world. When I stopped seeing my life as a never-ending melodrama, *it no longer was.* When I started looking for people to trust, I found them. When I stopped allying myself with emotionally unstable people, my world got healthier.

Over several years, with the help of my Jedi Master Jesse and my family, I *drove myself sane*, and—guess what?—it felt like the world was getting sane right along with me! That perspective was mostly just my own perception, but the immediate environment in *my own world* did become more sane, and I did everything I could to help that condition spread.

In the BAP, I got an incredible crash course in the predictable cause-and-effect mechanics of human nature, as my life improved immeasurably—even among my family and friends. The approach hinged on one powerful principle: If you do A with someone, you'll usually get B—whether you want to or not, work hard or not, or apply resources or not. People are people. Therefore: People are predictable.

I rode that principle all the way to the top of the program, and never looked back. In 2011, I was appointed head of the BAP. I was only its fourth leader in history, so I took the job very seriously. I felt obligated to leverage the most potent power I'd ever had into making America feel safe again.

I loved my new job. Time glided by with the peace of mind that comes naturally when you accept the fact that almost everything that people do—*from their perspective*—makes sense! (It may *suck*, but it makes sense.)

And if it makes sense, *you can predict it.*

And if you can predict it, *you can act accordingly.*

And then, far more often than not, the things people do won't even suck—especially in *your own* world—because you'll see them coming and can deal with them appropriately.

When people master that simple set of rules—as *you* probably have by now—they can easily become a resource for the success of others, which elevates their own success, as they form more and more alliances.

At that point, virtually all good things seem within reach.

December 2011
Saddam Hussein's Rec Room

"Do me a favor?" It was Jesse calling, shortly after I'd become head of the Behavioral Analysis Program.

"Name it."

He said he was calling on behalf of a young New York agent who felt like she was in over her head. She'd approached him because he was a legend at simplifying complex challenges.

Jesse was retired, but still helped the agency as a contract specialist, and was embedded with her squad. She was working Russia, which was raising all kinds of hell again.

This time the issue was: Would Russia become a genuine democracy, or regress once more into the kind of criminal dictatorship that had haunted the nation for three hundred years? (Spoiler alert: Don't get your hopes up.)

Vladimir Putin had just pulled off a rigged election that had triggered rioting in the streets and mass incarcerations, including the arrests of about a thousand political prisoners.

Even the concept of Russian political prisoners created terrible images in my mind, and I longed to help.

Russia has never abandoned the use of torture and terror, and there was no doubt that they were used in this situation. Some people lived to talk about it, and some didn't. The details are too disturbing to recount here.

The endless spiral of arrests, interrogations, imprisonment, abuse, and merciless intimidation of victims and their families that began then *is still happening*.

The agent Jesse called about was a young New York woman named Linda, who had recently earned a PhD in psychology. She'd just been briefed by another three-letter agency in NYC, and he'd pointed her toward a target who was suspected of running the current media whitewash of Russia's sadistic brutality. He supposedly worked at the

Russian consulate and the United Nations, but he had a background in media, and seemed to know the soft spots in the American psyche. The program Russia was using at this time was almost exactly the same strategy it had employed during the Chechen War: Blame Middle Eastern terrorists.

But to get to the target, Linda needed to take a circuitous path, through an Iraqi defector who'd reportedly worked directly with Saddam in his Baghdad palace. He wasn't a CHS, but we had reason to believe he might help us. He was attending a series of brown-bag lectures at Fordham University on Russian history—and so was the target.

Linda was freaked out, Jesse said, by the life-or-death elements of the case, even though the deaths were occurring thousands of miles away. The mission was a far cry from the cases of depression and anxiety she'd treated as a clinical psychologist before signing on with the FBI in order to, as she later put it, "make a difference."

"I told her I could teach her by example," Jesse said, "but that *you* could show her a system that she can keep using forever. She needs something like that."

Then he said softly, "She's not"—he hesitated—"functioning at her best." That was as close as he ever got to criticizing people. He generally expressed negativity by what he *didn't* say, which packed more punch than the explicit attacks of most people.

Jesse said that Linda had the potential to be a great agent, but that she was very sensitive, and her emotions seemed to be taking over. Her feelings were crowding out her rationality, and making her hesitant about what to do.

"Tell her I'd be happy to help," I said.

My plan was to do a standard BAP consultation: invite her—and her team, if possible—to Quantico, and help her create a strategy based on behavioral analysis. We'd try to discern the predictable behavior of the people involved, and offer suggestions, and points to consider. The execution of it, as always, would be up to the agent in charge: her, in this case.

For starters, I was concerned about the Iraqi that she needed to interview. He sounded like a spooky guy with a cloudy past.

There was some vague mention of him being the only man in Iraq that Saddam had feared—even though Saddam had his own torture chamber in the basement of the palace where he lived with his wife and kids. Saddam wanted it there because he *enjoyed* his own version of a rec room, just as his sons enjoyed their own rape rooms. He also had one in Manhattan, across the street from Michael Bloomberg's home, deep in the basement of the Mission of Iraq, where he authorized the kidnapping and abuse of Iraqis living in the U.S., using them for leverage against family members who were still in the Middle East. The torture chamber remained until federal investigators raided the building following Saddam's fall in 2003.

There were similar rooms in Iraqi embassies all around the world.

I could see how this level of horror might make Linda feel off-balance. Russia was successfully executing the most repulsive shift toward tyranny in recent history, and when you're that close to depravity, paranoia can chill your blood and make every possible fear seem dreadfully real.

Linda's reaction wasn't even unusual. Many people quickly become unstable in dangerous and hostile environments. And most people act irrationally when they're desperate. You never *really know* somebody until you see them try to function under fire.

But threatening events aren't even the most common cause of erratic, unpredictable behavior. Even people in typical, unremarkable environments can be pushed toward irrationality by many different factors: childhood abuse (which often prompts rebound abuse), adult PTSD, serious biochemical imbalances, substance abuse, head injuries, and neurological illnesses.

Even more people exist in a gray area of emotional instability that is not obvious, constant, nor even severe. These people are often expected to function as well as people with robust mental health, but they just can't.

Fortunately, though, other powerful factors can help people who "go crazy" to "go sane" again. These healing forces include medication, healthier lifestyles, counseling, the help of friends and family, meditation, support groups, spiritual fulfillment, and substance abuse treatment.

Those forces—of personal redemption and generous support—are among the most highly evolved functions of humanity. They allow us to remain stable in an unstable world, and to help others *regain* their stability.

Even so, emotional instability—even if temporary—is a hell of a monkey wrench to throw into the pursuit of predictable, laudable behavior.

The lack of emotional stability is arguably the most important deficit in all of the six signs—because it makes unstable people so hard to predict. Like everybody else, unstable people do what they *think is in their own best interests*, even if it isn't, which can set them off on a cycle of reckless or irrational behavior—which cannot be predicted.

Even more problematic, anyone with significant emotional instability usually destroys their ability to engage effectively in any of the other signs for predicting people.

So without the foundation of emotional stability, it can be very hard for people to properly exercise the other five signs, and they become virtually unknowable.

The best way to navigate that ocean of the unknown is to learn to spot emotional instability, and stay as far from it as possible, unless you feel morally obligated to help.

If I saw significant instability in Linda, I'd probably have to help her explore a role that was more suited to her. That's not quite like, "You're fired," but that's almost certainly how she'd see it.

January 2012
Second Impressions

In early January, Linda walked uncertainly into my office, exuding an attitude of: *I do not belong here.*

My first thought was: *Damn! This woman looks about as old as Dora the Explorer! Who's going to take* her *seriously? Russian spies?*

But I've learned that second impressions are almost always more accurate than the overrated first impression, because you've had time to *think*. Going with your gut is popular, but I guarantee you that your brain is smarter than your gut.

"Linda! Great to see you!"

I shook her hand, and it was cold. Nonverbal explanation: fear. Everybody knows that "cold feet" refers to fear—not just figuratively, but also literally, since fear constricts blood vessels, and impedes circulation to the extremities. But many people don't know that cold *hands* are just as indicative of fear, and are much harder for someone to conceal in a social situation. (So if you're going into a scary meeting, put your hands under warm running water, which masks your nervousness to anyone whose hand you might shake, as a *literal* expression of the fight-flight-freeze response. It sends your brain a feed-forward message of reassurance, the same way that taking a deep breath does.)

"Thanks for seeing me," Linda said, in sort of a little-girl voice that fit her appearance, but was almost certainly a career handicap.

She was breathing hard and said something apologetic about traffic.

I smiled, waved it off, and said, "Take a breath!"

I took one myself, because I was, to some extent, absorbing some of her fear, and coming up with stuff of my own to worry about. It's a natural instinct. Fear is the most contagious of all feelings—much more than love—because it's stored not just in the thought-dominated, rational forebrain, but in the even deeper regions of the primitive, mammalian brain, and even the reptilian brain.

But I was here for Linda, so I put my thoughts on rewind, and looked at her again. The single best way for me to achieve emotional stability in a relationship—and also to recognize stability in others—is to *see people as they are*, without emotional bias. Something trivial—such as simply having a youthful face or a high voice—may make someone different from me, but it was nothing more than a challenge to overcome. Unfortunately, though, difference is the underlying trigger of *most phobias*, and creates the multifaceted, broad-spectrum fear known as xenophobia. So it's not always easy to feel comfortable with people who are clearly different from you.

Even so, most of us don't need to be victims of *any* phobias, if we simply allow rationalism to lead the way.

Besides, I didn't want to let my own concerns make Linda feel even worse. How we feel, even when we think it's not obvious, has a powerful effect on how others feel—especially people who are already unstable. Their tipping point is too easy to reach.

So I took another breath, and looked at her again, trying to see her for who she was, without imposing my own prejudices.

She looked better! Older! Wiser! (Kids grow so fast!)

I asked her how I could be a resource for her, because vesting in someone's success is a phenomenally fast and effective way to gain an ally, and prompt people to open up.

She didn't really respond, though. Maybe she just felt helpless, and needed me to reach out even further. The best thing you can do with most people is to just keep trying.

"Jesse thinks you've got huge potential," I said. She seemed very flattered and relieved. I don't use fake flattery—people smell it a mile away—but I rarely see people who think they don't deserve a sincere compliment, even if it's a little exaggerated (because it rarely seems like an exaggeration to *them*).

I told her that I'd worked Russia for about twenty years, knew the culture, and that she could count on my help for as long as she needed it. As always, I sought her thoughts and opinions, validated her context, spoke in terms of her priorities, and empowered her with choice.

I trust you know the power of that approach by now.

She warmed up, but she was still scared. She had to go meet the Iraqi contact the following day. "I'll go with you tomorrow," I said.

Her nonverbals told me that much of her fear had just evaporated.

"I'll frame it to my supervisor as an urgent request for an informal consultation. Know why?"

She shook her head.

"Less paperwork."

For the first time, she smiled.

Long Island, New York
The Only Man Saddam Hussein Feared

The next day, as we drove out to Long Island to see the Iraqi, she was tense again. I knew that the stress, from a medical perspective, was impairing her cognitive function, including her memory and rationality. It's arguably the best single reason to control your emotions.

The man's house was nice—red brick with forest green shutters, and kids playing in the street—and it calmed my nerves a little. His wife answered the door. "Yeah?" she said. It reminded me of how Leo's grandson had answered the phone every time his caller ID showed it was me—at least in the early days.

I told her who we were and that we had an appointment with her husband.

"We'll see," she said, and closed the door.

We could hear her raise her voice. After some time, the man came out and started sizing us up. I put on my happy face, Linda was charming, and we managed to get in the door. I felt, as I often did, like a salesman—which was basically what I was. One way or another, we're all in sales, and like all salespeople, what we need to sell first is ourselves.

I brought up the class he was taking at Fordham University, because that was his link to our target. At the dining room table, I edged into understanding him better, so I could strategize a dialogue. But his wife suddenly appeared and shouted, "Oh my God—you're invading our privacy!"

Linda looked stunned. I gave her a look that said, *Don't buy into the drama.*

"I'm sorry, ma'am," I said, "but your husband invited us here. We'll leave if you want."

"You have no right!" She cited a law, and said she worked with the American Civil Liberties Union. I figured it had probably been a big stretch for her to go from Saddam's palace to the ACLU, so I shrugged it off.

The man stood, took her by the arm, and asked her to let Linda and me finish, as he guided her toward the door—to the best of his ability.

She barged in two more times, pissed and weird, and after the second time he escorted her out, we gave him a high-speed rundown on gathering some information about the presumed Russian spy. We could hear her just outside the door.

"I regret I cannot help you," he said.

Linda's expression went sour. I shook my head almost imperceptibly—meaning, *Don't let him emotionally hijack you.* Then I said to him, "Why? Are you concerned it's dangerous?"

"Yes," he said, motioning with his thumb toward the kitchen door. "But take this." He wrote down a phone number and the name Susan, and handed it to me. It seemed as if that had been his plan all along. "She, too, takes the class. She is very intelligent. Perhaps she would find this work . . . easier to schedule."

I gave the number to Linda, to help underscore her power for the Iraqi (and herself). I've found that if you hand off power often enough, the person you give it to will begin to feel and act empowered—not necessarily because you changed their degree of power, but because you acknowledged it. We're all pretty powerful, unless someone is trying to control us—and even then, most people rise to the occasion and make themselves heard.

We heard a pan hit the floor, probably to remind us that his wife was still home.

At that point, I had nothing to lose, so I said, "I heard something about you being the only man in the world that Saddam Hussein feared." I was just curious. I thought maybe he was some kind of secret police hitman—the kind of thug who emerges from nowhere during a coup, then disappears forever.

He smiled. "Yes. He did fear me. I'm surprised you know that."

"Why?"

I braced myself for a potentially chilling answer. Out of the corner of my eye, I saw Linda do the same.

"I was his dentist," he said.

We heard, "Shit!" from the kitchen. And another pan.

"I, too, fear only one person," he said. He used his thumb again, to finish the thought.

The Quiet Mind vs. the Noisy Mind

I subscribe to the psychological theory that there are only two basic emotions that are hardwired into the brain, and are the ultimate drivers of human thought and behavior: the opposing forces of love and fear.

All other emotions, in the end, are derived from them.

Even the deeply held emotion of anger, for example, comes from fear, because anger—in all its ferocity, and with all its comorbid conditions, such as hate or panic—commonly subsides and can even disappear when there is *nothing left to fear from whatever caused the anger*. Similarly, sadness—which most often comes from loss—is, at rock bottom, the fear of living forever without whatever is gone and will never return. The same basic principle of feeling relief when a threat is gone also applies to the other forms of fear, such as disgust, cynicism, distress, contempt, or insecurity.

Love, the other primary emotion that we're born with, emerges in its own forms of expression, including romance, security, protectiveness, appreciation, loyalty, enchantment, devotion, worship, and allegiance. And sometimes love is necessary to survive, and fear is necessary to thrive. They run that deep.

Fear is necessary to survive, and love is necessary to thrive. The same can't be said of any other single emotion.

The most beautiful thing about love—first widely proposed by prominent Duke University psychologist and author Dan Baker, PhD—is that it is mentally and emotionally impossible to be in a state of fear and a state of love at the same time. Love, therefore, is life's only reliable, eternal, and universal antidote to fear.

Love, in the broadest sense of the word, must also be present for trust. As I've delineated several times, there's a huge difference between liking or even *loving* someone, and trusting them. Trusting and liking are not at all synonymous. But they are in almost all cases simultaneously present, simply because trusting someone is impossible without a certain feeling of allegiance or identification, even if it comes only from having corresponding goals. It's also hard to see someone engage in the first sign of trust—vesting in your success—without feeling at least a little gratitude, which is essentially the same as appreciation, the all-giving, highest form of love.

Because of this, the conflicting emotions of love and fear are at the root of almost all the tells of emotional stability and instability.

I think of these two polarized conditions—love and emotional stability vs. fear and emotional instability—as the "quiet mind" vs. the "noisy mind." The quiet mind speaks with a single, consolidated voice, calmed by reason, while the noisy mind is often a cacophony of contradictory feelings, ungoverned by rationality, and muddled with emotion.

Love is the pure essence of the quiet mind, and fear is the constant cold shriek of the noisy mind.

The problem that blocks many people from achieving a quiet mind begins with the unavoidable fact that we are all descended from ancestors who learned to be survivors. Every single person who is now alive comes from a genetic lineage in which every ancestor from time immemorial not only survived, but gave birth to new life: humans who became stronger and smarter for generation after generation, ending with *you*.

How? With survival skills embedded deeply in the most primitive part of the brain. We're *built* for it—hardwired for hard times. We're endowed with genetic coding that urges us to put our own needs first, to seize power in each moment, and to remember insults and threats. That's the function of the noisy mind.

But over the millennia, we learned to override this genetic coding and organize our actions around the needs of *others*—an act that, paradoxically, provides the ultimate protection. That sense of social responsibility is a function of the quiet mind, which resides in the brain's most advanced area—the forebrain, near the forehead—and governs all rational thought.

The more primitive noisy mind is dominated by the very back of the brain, behind the forebrain and the mammalian brain, in the area known as the reptilian brain. It sits just above the spinal column, and mostly just handles automatic action and fear. It does very little thinking, but lots of neural housekeeping, like breathing and heartbeat. But those can be handy, too.

Virtually every element of trust is guided by the quiet mind, because the act of trusting people is—*or should be*—a thoughtful process. People who feel safe enough to assign trust rationally—and therefore effectively—have the ability to see others the way they are, rather than the way they *want* them to be. When you see people the way they are, you can see *yourself* the way *they* see you. When that happens, your assessment of their behavior becomes flawless—perfectly predictable— and together you can achieve great things.

The opposite outlook, driven by the fear found in the noisy mind, is animated by instinct and impulse, and is responsible for greed, compulsion, envy, and insecurity.

The survivor-based mindset is especially hard for type-A people to avoid, and they tend to become immune to the havoc they create, and the harm they do to themselves in the name of advancement. They sometimes dominate entire societies, but still do harm.

Ironically, one manifestation of the noisy mind—a fear-based feeling of unchecked egotism, and the choices made in its wake—is often a direct result of success. This subversive trait can be very hard to avoid. It's common for people to be blind to their own arrogance. The first sign they see often comes when others pull away. But by then it's often too late to repair the relationships.

Another unfortunate product of the noisy mind that's hard to avoid is the destructive habit of assigning negative labels to the person you're trying to size up. To predict people accurately, you can't even *think* in terms of someone being a liar, a manipulator, a cheat, or a betrayer. Most people have an uncanny ability to know when they're being judged, even when no judgments are voiced. These judgments, besides alienating people, can actually spur people to *adopt* the negative behaviors that they are suspected of having. When derogatory categories are assigned to people, I can't always tell what they will do, but I can predict a negative response with almost 100 percent accuracy.

Another failure of the noisy mind is to trust too much or too little.

Both behaviors stem from the single most common destructive force in business and in life: fear. People trust too much because they're apprehensive about facing challenges alone, and people are too wary of trust because they're worried that others will take advantage.

Most incorrect choices in predicting trust in someone are due to their *fear*—of not having enough or not being good enough—even if only in fear's familiar disguises of greed, vanity, envy, authoritarianism, anger, insecurity, and perfectionism. One of the most common ways fear asserts itself is in anxiety about rejection from one's own coworkers, supervisors, and even family and friends—in effect, one's "tribe."

Despite the power of the noisy mind, it can generally be overridden by the quiet mind, which has a multitude of fear-fighting factors. To state the obvious, the quiet mind is smarter than the noisy mind.

The outlook of the quiet mind is characterized by calmness and confidence, with the ability to see things realistically, and the discipline to avoid self-deceit, with its many traps, including unrealistic optimism.

The quieter your brain becomes, the more easily you'll recognize opportunities to move your goals forward in a seamless and easy manner.

Achieving this mindset is one of the great challenges of predicting behavior, and requires people to lead themselves to it. That's why another phrase I use to describe the actions of the quiet mind is "self-leadership."

Like other primary aspects of personality, the quiet mind is individualized and self-sponsored, and can't be created by other people unless you offer them your consent and active participation.

When you are assessing people for their most deep-seated behaviors, it's very important to look for the people who have the qualities of the quiet mind.

But nobody is perfect, and people should not be distrusted or disliked just because they're naturally pessimistic, insecure, or depressed—especially if they make an honest effort to refrain from acting out their troubled feelings on *you*. When they do have moderate emotional flaws—as *so many* of us do—you can still trust them, by establishing a baseline of their behavior, and being alert for deviations from that norm. For example, if you propose an idea to someone who is typically pessimistic, it's not necessarily a problem if they're pessimistic about your idea. It's just how they are, and they may have some interesting things to say about the idea, even if it's limited to potential problems.

Emotional stability exists on a continuum, and most people are adequately stable, while others have abundant emotional stability, characterized by self-control, consistency, communication skills, empathy, and the golden, self-sustaining quality of empathy that's combined with stoical acceptance, which I call stempathy.

Paradoxically, however, many people in our current compartmentalized, mechanized culture—particularly in the technological sectors—are skewed toward *overreliance* on rationality and emotional control, and have difficulty operating outside their narrow emotional bandwidth.

But who knows which of them will become the next dot-com billionaire? And whoever that may be will probably find that people are quite willing to talk to them, about whatever they want.

TEN NEGATIVE TELLS FOR EMOTIONAL STABILITY

1. People learn to be helpless. We're all born helpless, but some people seem to get *better* at it as they age. At first, it's not because they want to, but because they get stuck in insoluble situations that they seemingly have no control over. Most people keep trying—but not everybody.

Some people respond to this as if it's a valid life lesson: You're helpless—in *every* situation!

That conclusion may seem ridiculous, but it's very common, and results in a trait called "learned helplessness."

The desire among people with learned helplessness to give up in difficult situations can become a deeply held trait. It's so instinctual that it even occurs in animals.

2. People surrender their right to positive perceptions. People can be born with mood chemistry that's so skewed that it darkens their perceptions.

Trauma can also create mood disorders, including depression and anxiety.

But in many cases among people who are consistently negative, there is no organic cause of a mood disorder, nor evidence of significant trauma.

It appears to simply be a choice.

It's a bad choice—and often a lazy one—and with persistent freezing behavior—also called "dissociation"—the choice can become as immovable as an iceberg.

When someone perceives life as inherently negative, they are hard to predict, because they've usually lost touch with their goals. They're like the *Titanic* (a metaphor I keep coming back to): big ships with tiny rudders. It's particularly dangerous in iceberg country.

When they don't know what they want, you don't know, either, and then it becomes very hard to trust them, vest in them, or perceive a long relationship.

3. People catastrophize. Some people have an extremely low tolerance for problems, and have a hard time sorting big problems from little ones. To them, almost every problem looks like a fearful catastrophe.

Their expectations have a way of fulfilling themselves, especially when other people are involved, since fear is one of the most contagious of all emotions. It is very difficult to trust people who think every little thing is a disaster. They're out of control, and totally unpredictable.

Even so, you can establish their negative attitude as their baseline behavior, and then interpret their reactions accordingly. When you accept the stoic reality that most things simply *are*—without judging them as good or bad—you can often deal successfully with damaged people.

4. People show signs of the "3-P" personality. It harbors three toxic traits: permanence, pervasiveness, and personalization.

Permanence is thinking that today's problem will be there forever. These people deserve kindness, but kindness need not translate into trust and partnership. So be kind, but beware.

Pervasiveness is thinking that a problem in one part of your life is sure to infect other parts. But that usually doesn't happen, so if you can't talk somebody out of it, don't trust them with something important—or you may become their *next* problem.

Personalization is assuming that every problem is your own fault—even the weather, as in: "I should have known it would rain. When will I ever learn?" Don't get sucked into this vortex of negative self-absorption. Try to steer clear of anybody who has a full-blown 3-P personality.

But you can help people, as I mentioned, to go sane. That's achieved through kindness, patience, practical help, insight, and the tough-love quality of empathy plus stoicism that I call stempathy. However, if somebody has multiple, connected, self-destructive instabilities, the smart thing to do is to limit your interaction with them in serious matters.

5. People perceive themselves as victims. I'm not one of those people who deny the existence of victimization. It's all around us.

Even so, countless people habitually feel sorry for themselves, despite only *mild* suffering. It's based in fear, and can limit the lives of not only the self-professed victims, but those who try to help them.

That's not hard-hearted. It's rational—and it's the best way to have the energy to help the people who really need it.

6. People have a sense of entitlement. Keep your eyes open, especially at work, for people who seem *too* carefree, have time to waste, and don't get much done. They are the entitled.

They may be amusing and charming, because those qualities come easily to the well rested, but every day that you get stronger, they get weaker.

Affiliation, respect, and trust belong to those who have something to offer, or it's not win-win—and if it's not win-win, it won't last.

7. People wait to be rescued. This is another toxic behavior of the modern era. Self-reliance is out of style.

Overdependence upon others is contrary to *human* nature, and the very laws of nature itself.

All creatures are provided with almost every resource they need, but the resources that nature offers must be gleaned, developed, divided, and stored. There's no way around it.

The demand for emotional rescue is even more common than the demand for physical rescue, and is just as insidious.

The hidden tragedy is that the rescuer is almost always overly idealized, and is expected to keep it up. If you don't, you'll be the new villain!

8. People think blame is constructive, because it exposes the weak links, and keeps people on their toes.

But it's really the ugly flip side of rescue. It's a way of finding another person to take responsibility for what happens to you.

Start with the fact that whoever screwed up knows it, and feels worse than anyone.

Most people realize that scapegoating is wrong, but fail to see that finding the "right" person to punish is quite similar. Efficient functioning depends solely upon *getting the job done,* not singling out the person who failed. It's only good for venting, feeling superior, creating grudges, generating fear, and encouraging people to lie.

Don't ally yourself with somebody who thinks blame is an efficient mechanism for optimal function. You could be next.

9. People are volatile. But they're not stupid, so sometimes they'll leaven their angry volatility with something positive, but equally inappropriate. They'll celebrate a moderate victory as if it's world-changing, or they'll promote somebody in a fit of grandiose generosity. From their perspective, they're exuberant, ultratransparent, and spontaneous.

They're actually just emotionally unstable, and get off on inflicting their mood swings and psychological imbalance on the people around them.

It enables them to retain their narcissistic position as the center of attention.

But if you like walking on eggs, it's fine.

10. People are manipulators. If they're good manipulators, you won't even notice until it's too late. They'll treat you great, then grab something you deserve, leave you out of an alliance, or just make you look bad.

If they're really good, you won't have a single opportunity to correct the damage they've done to you.

Manipulation is the antithesis of productive, positive behavior. In a C-suite setting, it's the pure essence of the power paradox.

Their ultimate goal may be to provoke you, but there is one thing they can't control: your reaction.

You can learn about the dark side of human behavior from them, but stay as far away as possible.

August 2012
Linda: Trusted Associate

"Two weeks left and I'm outta here!" Linda said. "That's the bad news—for you. *I'm* okay with it!"

Linda was funny. And a great FBI agent. But now I was going to lose her, because she'd landed a teaching job at a prestigious California university. Made me sad. She was supplying good information on her Russian target, and we'd both learned from each other.

She took me deeper into behavioral psychology than any of my course instructors had, and it gave me a theoretical foundation for the techniques I now apply in the real world. I'd taught her to distrust the noisy-mind messages that she'd once considered a key element of critical thinking.

For about a year, we'd gotten together or talked on the phone every couple of weeks, and she'd given me everything she had on a small coterie of Russians, through her CHS named Susan, the woman who knew the Iraqi dentist. Susan saw most of them almost every week, usually at the ongoing lectures at Fordham.

It looked to me as if Linda's original target, as I'd suspected, was spreading disinformation about the protests in Russia, and the victims of Putin's police state. I was noticing a lot of articles, news conferences, think tank reports, news clips, and print ads about the Russian campaign against "domestic terrorists."

The name of the diplomat—Adrik Petrov, let's say—was never attached to any of the releases about Chechnya, but it all originated in the New York Russian consulate, where he worked.

We had determined that Adrik had filled the slot of a diplomat who had clandestinely worked in intelligence, and Linda had discovered that he'd also replaced a spy in London several years prior. Adrik didn't tell her the guy was a spy, but he'd mentioned the name and we'd confirmed his role, so I wanted to get as much as I could.

But now she was leaving.

"Gonna miss you," I said.

"Me, too. I owe you one. I was seriously down on myself when we met. So many pressures to act a certain way, and say the right things. It carried over into my whole life. But you showed me I could act like myself, and if somebody had a problem, it was *their* problem."

"Thanks," I said. "But I just saw what was there already. It's *you. You* did it."

"Still owe you one. And here it is. I've got an idea," Linda said. "I'll have Susan launch it. She's leaving town, too—for real. She'll tell Adrik that she's met somebody—a guy who works for investment bankers in

Eastern Europe—who's looking for ground truth for investors, and that she's been writing research reports for them. The 'investor' will be one of my people—or *you*, if you'd prefer."

"Don't say 'ground truth,'" I said. "It's spy-talk."

"Okay, 'inside information.' Susan will tell Adrik she's leaving town and needs to have somebody cover for her during the next few months. She'll ask Adrik if he'll do it, as a favor to her. They're pretty tight. Susan likes him. Doesn't trust him, but likes him. She'll tell him that it's a really good gig, with big money floating around. He'll see it as a chance to grab more information. Susan told me he'll probably do it anyway, because he's a nice guy."

Linda said other complimentary things about him, and it worried me a little, because her descriptions of him didn't fit the profile of a spy. For one thing, Russians like their spies to be extreme risk takers, because they want them to *take extreme risks*. The FBI has the opposite perspective. They don't like risk takers, since they're too likely to flame out. Adrik was more like an FBI guy. Linda thought he was just conflict-avoidant.

She also said the only thing he didn't like about being a diplomat was the "importance" of the job, which she interpreted as "power." She said he worried about not giving his aides and office staff enough of what they needed, and that once he'd had to fire a guy and had almost quit himself.

I thought about Linda's idea for minute. "You're good," I told her.

"I know." She was matter-of-fact, not boastful.

Three weeks later, I was in an overpriced steak house on the East Side, not too far from the United Nations, with Adrik Petrov.

Adrik was about my age, was thin and fit, and he seemed to be observant, glancing around the restaurant in the seemingly distracted but very focused manner of a Secret Service agent, or personal bodyguard. He was wearing a black suit and white shirt, and I was impressed by its simplicity. We were in a style-heavy neighborhood that was often *too* heavy. I was dressed better than usual, because I was supposed to be one of the rich guys who wanted inside information.

After we ordered, I tried to steer the conversation to the new wave of protests in Russia, but he was clearly uncomfortable. "I saw too much of conflict. In the streets," he said. "When I was young. Those were bad days. It was after I got home from the Afghan War and the Soviet Union was dissolving. Life should have been good." He was lost in thought, and suddenly seemed more interested in his steak. We stopped talking, and he seemed comfortable with silence.

He wasn't as I'd imagined, and I could see why Susan had connected with him. Sometimes you just can't get a fix on somebody until they're sitting right in front of you, and then you can read them like a map. A word of advice: Don't live in the e-world 24/7. Go face-to-face at every reasonable opportunity.

"Susan said you have business interests in Eastern Europe," Adrik said.

"I do. I need to be cautious about revealing what they don't wish to be public, but they are substantial people with many interests."

Instead of following up on that, Adrik went back to the subject of Susan. That was interesting. Most people, when given the chance to talk about money or a mutual acquaintance, will talk about the money.

I realized he had no interest in doing business, but was just doing a favor for Susan.

I asked Adrik about his family, and he brightened. His two children, he said, were coming to New York for the remainder of his tour here. He didn't mention anything about a wife.

I started talking about my own kids, and he seemed genuinely interested, but I wanted the focus to return to him.

It never did. That was all I got. Happens all the time.

We met a few more times, and he gave me some written information that I requested. It was very precise, and quickly worked its way up the Bureau hierarchy.

It got me noticed, and put the BAP in a favorable light.

Not every relationship leads to glory, but in the end, those that do and those that don't can be hard to tell apart.

TEN POSITIVE TELLS FOR EMOTIONAL STABILITY

1. People show an abundance of appreciation. If the two most primal emotions are love and fear—with love leading the way to emotional stability—appreciation is pure elixir of emotional stability, because it is the finest form of love. It is the outward-flowing, self-perpetuating aspect of love that gives everything, and asks for nothing.

As such, it is the single most potent force against fear—and fear is the worst enemy of emotional stability.

When someone is in a state of appreciation, they are literally incapable of feeling fear. The two states are mutually exclusive.

Appreciation makes not only the giver, but also the recipient, far more capable of attaining the courage that creates bold visions and life-changing relationships.

2. People are hard to scare. Fearlessness is the single most natural companion of appreciation, and is indispensable for people who are trying to inspire your trust.

Fearlessness is even greater than the very similar quality of courage, because courage is the ability to *overcome* fear, while fearlessness indicates an *absence* of fear.

The condition of fearlessness cannot be constant, because fear is not only endemic to the human race, but also indispensable.

But a little fear goes a long way.

Fearless people are usually fun and effective, and can be genuinely inspiring.

In an age of constantly churning crises, fearless people rise above the fray and are virtually immune to one of the great saboteurs of trust: desperation.

3. People are impeccably rational. Rationality is in shockingly short supply in an era dominated by emotion. Our society is now almost bereft of the once common checks and balances of an unbiased media, and a dedication to civil discourse, and that has taken a terrible toll on rationality.

Those who treasure it, though, have a big head start on being trustworthy, because it's easy to predict what they'll do in almost any rational scenario. Rationality is governed by *rules*: very old rules, which have the same basic application now as they did eons ago.

Rationality, like love, is also one of our strongest forces against fear, since fear is an emotion that arises from the most primitive part of the brain.

The most incredible "wiring" in the human brain dictates that 95 percent of all incoming information goes straight to the brain's most advanced portion—the forebrain—and only then is shipped to the fear-driven part of the brain.

Many people don't take advantage of that gorgeous work of wiring. And then they wonder why they're regarded as a loose cannon, with very few allies.

4. People adhere to the Code of Trust. Even if they've never heard of it, they have intuitively adopted its five principles as a practical and ethical part of their behavioral code. When you find somebody who does that, you're good to go: They're among the easiest people in the world to trust.

They've put a lid on their ego. They validate people by taking the time to understand them, by finding some common ground. They don't judge people, so they get to hear almost everything. They're reasonable and rational, which makes them predictable, even in the worst crisis. And they're generous enough to always go win-win.

Use that decoding method, and you'll never fail to meet the right people.

5. People offer you choices. What's not to trust? It's your choice, so it's hard to go wrong.

Having choice is what freedom is all about. It feels good, and it works even better.

Having limited choices feels like being in jail, and can come from something as common as just being micromanaged.

Self-autonomy is the path to self-esteem.

When people offer that to you, you feel like you live in *your* world—the one you've always wanted, where you're in charge—and you're in the company of the people who helped make it happen.

6. People are happy with themselves. That allows them to be happy with you. Nothing is worse than a relationship with people who don't like themselves. Sooner or later, they'll decide they don't like you, either.

It's not so easy to be happy with yourself. There are too many people who enjoy being critical of you. And there are also innumerable people in business, government, and culture who want you to feel inadequate, and in need of what they provide.

People who aren't satisfied with themselves are hard to satisfy. They undermine your efforts, even at the expense of their own. That creates classic cases of people who don't work in their own best interests. It makes them impossible to predict, and therefore impossible to trust as an ally.

People who aren't happy with themselves tend to be unemotional, negative, and critical, and they even direct a lot of their own sour attitude toward themselves.

People who like themselves tend to be pleasant, accepting, funny, and healthy. You know what they like and where they're headed, so it's easy to trust them, and build great alliances.

7. People have power, but don't love it. It's easy for trustworthy, centered people to rise to positions of power, because they're magnets for other positive people, and work with diligence and self-responsibility.

But they take little pleasure, if any, in the power they have over other people. Because of their suspension of ego, they don't pat themselves on the back for being able to tell other people what to do. For truly sane people, power is nothing more than a lot of work.

Why? Because they care about people, try to be fair, and like to serve as a resource for the success of others.

They may have a corner office, but many of them speak nostalgically of the days when they had fewer management responsibilities, and more time in the field.

These people are extraordinarily valuable as a force against the power paradox. For the power-paradox people, just *trying* to reach for power can doom their dream, because we all have a natural tendency to distrust someone who loves power.

Those who are truly worthy of power don't pursue it. It pursues them.

8. People are flexible. Life changes, and if you don't change with it, you get left behind. You'll pay for your rigidity with anxiety, dissociation, depression, and various practical penalties, such as loss of income, or outdated skills. All of this can quickly add up to desperation.

Because most desperate people will do almost anything to escape their peril, they're hard to predict.

Flexible people feel as if life has innumerable opportunities, so they're eager to accept new people, ideas, and places into their lives. They're open and reasonable with those who reach out to them, and see change as an opportunity, instead of a threat.

9. People are calm. This trait reflects fairness, friendliness, optimism, and generosity. As a rule, people like this are successful, because they're great in a crisis—and even better at not creating crises.

An old cliché is, "The bigger they are, the nicer they are." But behavioral studies show that this variation of that theme is also true: "The nicer they are, the bigger they are."

One study showed that "givers" are more likely to succeed than "takers."

Calm people function more effectively than hyperactive people, and are much easier to work with.

Part of their relaxed attitude comes from having no enemies, because they're nice to people, and attract trust.

It's good that we're motivated to trust nice people. It makes life feel far more sensible.

10. People don't look for problems. They don't need to. They don't feed on the drama that manipulators like, or play games of power.

Emotionally stable people look for the best in others, so they're usually the first to find it.

A businessperson I know who depends upon internet research in his job always starts his search by looking at sites that tell him what he wants to hear. That's not where the research ends, of course, but by starting with a search for good news, he remains optimistic, as he finds supporting information. Only then does he look for problems. If he started from the negative end, he says, he'd probably give up before he got to the bottom of the situation.

One interesting study about optimism in the workplace showed that optimistic people process information more effectively than people who feel negative or neutral, theoretically because a troubled mind is a greater distraction than a positive one.

Welcome to the Bureau!

Okay, I know you've figured out the anecdote in this chapter.

You know who I trusted, who I didn't, and why. You've learned to think like an agent.

You ignored the distractions caused by emotion.

- You were brutally honest.
- You didn't trust people just because you liked them.
- You resisted manipulation.
- You forgot about your own political leanings.
- You read between the lines.

But let's honor the process and break it down.

Adrik: What a nice guy! He turned out to be a straight-up diplomat, with nothing on his record but honor. You trusted him, Susan *almost* trusted him, and Linda kept an open mind, which was one of her greatest assets.

I finally did, too. We all came to that conclusion *in spite of* the fact that he was a nice guy.

We had to be tough, right? What kind of people would we be if we trusted someone just because he was nice, and allowed him to continue to be complicit in a propaganda program that tried to legitimize false imprisonment, torture, and occasional murder? The circumstantial case against Adrik—that he replaced spies in two different embassies, and was peripherally associated with a propaganda program—made him a person of interest, but that's all. He was a regular diplomat with nothing on his record but honor.

Let's look at his numbers. He was obviously a hard guy to scare (Positive Tell #2), because he'd fought in the plains of Afghanistan and served in a government that too often turned on its own.

He'd also seen enough of war to make him *rational* about it in the way that only those who have served can understand (Positive Tell #3), while millions of others who've never been near war see it almost as a spectacle, or even a sport.

Even before I met Adrik, I'd learned from Linda that he accepted power only as a burden (Positive Tell #7), that he was conflict-avoidant (Positive Tell #10), and that he was generous enough to work with her until she'd make the move to California (Positive Tell #4).

From the first time I met him, I could see that he had a very calm, nonvolatile personality (Positive Tell #9). I also noticed that he had no problem with what many people perceive as awkward silences during our conversations. It's been my observation that people who are like that feel very comfortable with themselves, and people who like themselves *the way they are* tend to stay that way, and are easy to predict (Positive Tell #6).

From the several other times I saw him, I never perceived even *one* of the negative tells of trust.

And you trusted Susan, didn't you? Hell yeah! You didn't get many details about her, but what you saw was a true patriot who operated efficiently, with nothing to gain for herself.

Linda: She's a little more complex. At first, when she seemed to be having an emotional crisis, we saw signs of learned helplessness (Negative Tell #1), the desire to be rescued (Negative Tell #7), and a propensity for catastrophizing (Negative Tell #3). I didn't trust her early on. If I had, I wouldn't have gotten as involved as I did. But when I offered help, stempathy, and patience, she practically became a different person. *Sometimes that's all it takes!* So remember that when you run into people you don't initially trust. Over time, as I soon predicted, she became calm (Positive Tell #9), happy with herself (Positive Tell #6), and rational (Positive Tell #3).

You probably trusted the dentist, too—despite his connection with Saddam Hussein—because you didn't have enough hard data to indicate that he was a willing accomplice to crime. All you knew was that he'd escaped from that situation at the first opportunity. So that act alone—a reflection of Sign #4: Actions—was sufficiently redemptive to trigger a tentative level of trust, especially since it was reinforced by positive, transparent communication (Sign #5: Language).

Trust the dentist's wife? Not so much. You undoubtedly observed her almost constant state of desperation—the "kryptonite" of trust—which was not consistent with *any* of her stressors of the moment. She seemed like the kind of person who would find a way to screw herself up. But you had plenty of data indicating that she'd been through quite an ordeal, and maybe was still healing. So you probably thought her PTSD was understandable, and predictable. She would have been scarier if she'd acted like Mrs. Perfect.

Now: Can you imagine trying to size these people up without my behavior assessment system?

I can't. I often wonder how I ever evaluated anybody with just the tools of conventional decision making: intuition, open-source research, legwork, libraries, and the opinions of various people, along with other surface-level information—some of which is often falsified, as so much is these days.

Around the time I met these people, I was applying my system on a virtually daily basis, and it became vastly easier to size people up and predict what they'd do.

As more operatives were neutralized, Americans gradually stopped hearing—and believing—that Russia's barbarism was a heroic battle against terrorists.

So hopefully the system helped to indirectly save some lives, at least, or stop some atrocities. But we'll never know. Fine with me. All that matters is that it stopped.

For the next six years, I became increasingly involved with the science and application of understanding people, and accurately predicting what they would do.

It gave meaning to my life in the FBI, and to the new life I began after I retired from the Bureau in 2018.

If the American public becomes interested in this rational way of evaluating other people, I think it will change the country. Or certain segments. Who knows?

If it ever happens, maybe you'll be part of it.

In this newly blossoming millennium, invigorated and informed by the new wave of people who feel most at home in history's newest era, you will search for the allies you need—protected by this system—as you offer prosperity and power to all who join you.

The search will enable you to *build your own life*—free from devastation, if you fall—and then *build it again*, as the positive people around you grow wiser, happier, more abundant, and closer, in a journey of humankind that will, with great good fortune, never end.

DEBRIEFING

CHAPTER 8:
"SEE INSIDE PEOPLE"

SIGN #6: STABILITY

Key Quote: "Most incorrect choices in predicting trust in someone are due to their *fear*—of not having enough or not being good enough—even if only in fear's familiar disguises of greed, vanity, envy, authoritarianism, anger, insecurity, and perfectionism."

Key Message: A lack of emotional stability is arguably the most devastating deficit in all of the six signs—because if somebody strays into emotional self-destruction just long enough to *stop pursuing their own best interests*, they're suddenly a loose cannon, and will be far harder to predict.

THE TAKEAWAYS

1. **Unmanageable problems:** Parts of our lives are often temporarily dominated by people who have problems they can't handle. These people act out their own issues in the public arena, and make

life more challenging for everyone. But they are very much in the minority, and their troubling actions are usually transparent.

2. **Emotional instability:** The two most common sources of emotional instability are biochemical imbalances and prior trauma. Both can be overcome, often with the help of other people. The help transforms what once was pain into a new level of love, both for the person who was helped and for the helper.

3. **Embracing imperfections:** When people realize that they're good enough as they are, they usually see that they're even better than they need to be. One last, ironic note to perfectionists: Don't worry about being perfect. Worry about being *good enough.* That does not mean being *just okay.* It means reaching a *high level of conduct and insight.* And there's even a good chance you've already done it.

Ten Positive Tells for Emotional Stability

1. They're very appreciative. Appreciation is the purest form of love, because it gives everything and asks nothing.

2. They're hard to scare. They have almost no free-floating anxiety that needs to be attached to some event, so they're on an even keel, even when things get hairy.

3. They're impeccably rational. Rationality is arguably the most underrated of all virtues.

4. They follow the Code of Trust. They're humble, nonjudgmental, rational, understanding, and generous, and these traits usually grow more vibrant as they grow older.

5. They offer you choices. Nobody likes to be ordered around, and people who know that get far *more* help and *more* kindness from others than those who insist on creating the illusion of control.

6. They're happy with themselves. So they're happy with you. When that happens, you can be yourself. When you're happy with yourself, you're happy with them, and the circle of contentment can begin again.

7. They don't relish the power they have. It's a burden to them, because they want to use it fairly and wisely. That's why people *want* them to have it.

8. They're flexible. Life is one long process of letting go. Some people see that as loss. Others see it as a constant source of rebirth and re-creation.

9. They're calm. They make sure that the quiet mind prevails over the noisy mind.

10. They don't *look* for problems, or act them out with others.

Ten Negative Tells for Emotional Stability

1. They learn to be helpless, and use it to manipulate.

2. They surrender their right to positive perceptions, without experiencing significant precursors, including biochemical imbalances or trauma.

3. They catastrophize, by exaggerating their problems and getting caught in the dissociative "freeze" condition of the fight-flight-freeze response.

4. They have a 3-P personality and believe that 1) every problem will last forever (permanence), 2) individual problems will spread to other parts of their lives (pervasiveness), and 3) they're personally at fault for every problem they have (personalization).

5. They fall prey to victimization, automatically labeling themselves as victims for most of the things in their lives that don't please them, no matter how minor.

6. They have a sense of entitlement. They think they're better than other people, and have a right to seize a disproportionate share of resources.

7. They wait to be rescued. It's easy, and it makes them feel good. If you offer to be their white knight, get used to it.

8. They blame others. It's another one of those things that makes insecure people feel better, so they tell themselves that it's for the good of everybody, including the person they blame.

9. They're volatile. One minute they're over-the-top angry and the next they're ridiculously positive. Either way, they're the center of attention.

10. They're manipulators. Instead of being forthright about what they want, they play mind games, and try to stay under the radar until all of the traps they set spring shut.

AFTERWORD
The Golden Moments

Choice and Change

Life rarely travels in a straight, unbroken line. As a rule, life's most important moments don't even unfold in gradual twists and turns, but at abrupt right angles, created by the choices we make: to trust or doubt, to accept or reject, to go or stay, to love or fear. These are the moments that define us.

Each binary choice occurs at a ninety-degree intersection, or at least a fork in the road, and every one of them creates not only the utterly unique "you" in your life, but also the equally singular world in which you live.

Making a healthy, rational choice forges a golden moment in your life, and a long series of them—each building upon the others—can reward you with a veritable dream life: one of happiness, prosperity, love, health, and gratitude.

Even so, for most people, this unrelenting procession of choices can be nerve-racking, overwhelming, and even paralyzing.

But for *you*—at this pivotal point in your exploration of ideas—it probably isn't. You've learned how to *predict the outcome* of your choices—rationally and dispassionately—with a simple, six-point system for sizing people up and enlisting them in your own self-selected future.

When your future is foreseeable, it's easy to make these choices. You know what you're doing and see where you're going. Your life proceeds gracefully, with minimal melodrama and very little waste of time, money, worry, or regret.

Why do you have this special advantage? *Because you've learned to think like an FBI behavioral analyst.* You know who to trust, and why. It's as if you can see inside people, knowing that what you see is what you get.

At this point, you're in the rare company of those who compose America's largest and—in my opinion—finest domestic investigative agency. With logic, discipline, and information, you can spot flakes and phonies, defy the forces of manipulation, get to the bottom of complex questions, and find the kind of allies that will supercharge your life.

It was a hard system to create, but as you've seen, it's easy to operate, if you can just remember six words:

THE SYSTEM FOR SIZING PEOPLE UP

1. Vesting

2. Longevity

3. Reliability

4. Actions

5. Language

6. Stability

This method of behavioral analysis—guided at each juncture by deductive reasoning—has freed you from the mind-numbing forces of emotion, distraction, trickery, coercion, false fears, false hopes, and desperation.

It's enabled you to clearly see the world as it *is*. From this fully informed starting place, you're in the perfect position to create not only your own life, but your *own world*, populated by your supporters, and customized to fit your own special abilities and desires.

You can't always change the world, but you usually can change *your* world.

The people who share your worldview will be happy to help you succeed, because it's in their best interests. They'll stick with you for the long haul and will help you do the work that keeps your alliance strong. They'll be competent and diligent, and will almost always know what to say—and what *not* to say. And they'll have enough emotional stability to let you sleep well at night and awake to a morning of promise and pleasure.

As you've discovered, most of your allies won't excel at all six of these behavioral cornerstones, but they don't need to. Nobody's perfect, but anybody who's proficient in at least one or two of these psychosocial graces can learn the others, since they're all so closely linked and synergistic.

When some of your allies can't be a resource for everything you need, other people will fill in for them. Platinum-level success doesn't always take a village, but it certainly takes a team.

The main reason you'll need a team is because *change* is a virtual *definition* of life (just as death is defined by immobility), and hitting a moving target can't be done by the proverbial Army of One.

Sadly, though, the people who are trapped in their own *living* immobility often perceive change as nothing but *loss*—almost as if it's a form of death. That's not much of a leap, because the specter of death is the strongest and longest-held fear of most people, and it's easy for these people to piggyback their living fears upon it.

This unhealthy linkage is hard to break, because change and death share a formidable link: fear of the unknown.

Tragically, when people make the transition from lifelong fear of change to the hush of the grave, it's as if they had never lived on this earth at all.

Can there be a *better* reason to learn predictability and embrace change?

There is—but only one: to luxuriate throughout life in an undulation of constantly cresting moments of gold.

But rising to that level and staying there isn't easy, because—again—nobody's perfect. Including me, of course.

January 7, 2019
Quantico, Virginia
Free at Last

I didn't feel like myself. Something was off, and I had a pretty good idea of what it was.

After thirty consecutive years of serving America—in the Marine Corps and FBI—I was free. That was the problem. Or so I thought.

This day—a Monday that was devoid of work, or even a bittersweet nostalgia for the weekend—should have felt like one of the best ever.

But I was sitting in a restaurant feeling gloomy, and waiting for my life to begin.

Some people in that situation—newly retired, and on the cusp of creating another career—would refer to their future as their "new" life, but to me it felt so foreign that it was like my *next* life: as if the old one had been in another universe, long ago.

So I was a little uneasy. The only certainty I had was that, from this point on, everything would look different. But, as you now know, I'm no longer afraid of change.

I'm not even particularly afraid of death anymore, or the inevitable changes that precede it. To me, all of that is just a challenge. An adventure!

But this would be my biggest change yet. And the finality of no longer being a marine or an FBI agent carried consequences that were hard to predict. It was, to some extent, an exploratory voyage into the void.

Some people believe in a very literal afterlife of heavenly bliss, and some think they'll rejoin the universe as something along the lines of a white light, or as another creature. Some believe in nothingness. What just about everybody agrees on, though, is that it's going to be *way different.*

Even so, while we're still alive, we all experience versions of our existence that for all practical purposes are completely new incarnations.

The starkest rendition of this is the passage from infancy to childhood, when our first memories of life are essentially erased into oblivion, an occurrence that neurologists call infantile amnesia. For some people, everything before about age ten fades to nothingness.

As life proceeds, this incremental loss continues, often quite consciously, as we abandon what we have to create a better version of what will be. With that loss—and the freedom that so often accompanies major change—old opinions, strategies, and alliances wither, just as surely as memories fade.

For all intents and purposes, therefore, all of us have already died— and not entirely metaphorically. With each passing day, part of us is gone, while the rest—and hopefully the best—moves on.

I'd spent years developing that philosophy of choice and change, and I thought it would make retirement a cakewalk.

Okay, fine . . . So *why*, then, was I so uneasy?

Was it just plain old lack of income? After all, money is the root of all freedom.

If that sounds questionable, or even cynical, ask any retiree who's sitting on a nice nest egg—or ask one who *isn't.* Ask anybody who works two jobs just to survive. Don't even bother asking the wealthiest one percent.

Money can't buy happiness or love—but it can buy time. And free time, governed solely by oneself, offers the richness of choice that ultimately constitutes freedom.

But not for me. I'm motivated far more by passion and patriotism than by money.

Maybe I missed the excitement of work. Sometimes my job was dicey and disturbing, but it never got boring.

I also might have been missing the loss of a palpable, immediate purpose. I was no longer a role, but just a man staring—without really seeing—into the void.

I did feel tired, not physically, but with a bone-deep psychic exhaustion from the endless effort of keeping other countries from ripping America apart—without us even knowing it—as we blamed each other for ugly things that hadn't even happened.

Even so, here I was, suddenly free from the routines that had limited my life for as long as I could remember—feeling strangely stifled and restrained, and missing something I couldn't name. *Why?*

"Robin!" It was Jesse Thorne.

"Obi-Wan!"

After Jesse retired from his post in New York, he'd moved down here, close to Quantico, Virginia. Lately he'd become fascinated by my system for sizing people up. He'd inspired at least half of it himself, but had always been a seat-of-the-pants, intuitive agent who didn't need a system. There are people like that, but I've only known a few.

I'd promised to lay the whole thing out for him when we both had time, and *now* that time was here.

The waiter brought out two beers: Goodwood Bourbon Barrel Stout, seasoned in whiskey barrels.

"So," Jesse said. "Sizing people up: What's the secret sauce?"

"You'll think it's too simple," I said. "It's just six things, and you know all of them."

"Humor me."

"Okay. Six signs." I took my first sip of stout, with a sense of wonder and guilt about drinking before dark. "If any one sign obviously applies to somebody, you can usually trust them. But more is better. To spot the sign, you just look at people objectively and rationally—the same way agents do—looking for tells."

"Tells like nonverbals? Intentions? Actions? Track record?"

"Yep. The basic investigative elements. The most important is when somebody vests their interests in your success. I learned that from Leo."

"Hell of a guy. On Putin's hit list!"

"Leo lived and died by his relationships," I said. "They were his money in the bank. He taught me that we're all salesmen, and that the only thing we have to sell is ourselves. If somebody buys you, they'll eventually buy what you've got. Leo was the one who introduced me to Sergei," I said. "Remember him?"

"Yeah, Russian diplomat. What made you trust Sergei?"

"Solid nonverbals, high emotional intelligence, good listener, looked for ways to expand the relationship, candid, transparent. Asked about my priorities. He didn't promise me anything, but when you trust somebody, you don't need promises. You can just let them be themselves—"

Jesse finished my sentence: "And they'll let you be you."

Old mentors never die; they just stay a step ahead.

"And Leo introduced me to Annan," I said.

"Annan! You served with him in World War III! Right? Except it was just the two of you."

"That's my kind of war."

"The best thing in counterintelligence is what *doesn't* happen."

"Annan taught me the second sign of trust: thinking that a relationship will have longevity," I said. "Right off the bat, he realized he and I could be a big help to each other on a lot of things over the years. So it was easy to trust him."

Jesse took a long pull on his Bourbon Barrel Stout and said, "What's the third sign?"

"Reliability—based on competence and diligence. I learned this one from what *not* to do, when I got hooked up with a drone team and our first job was organizing a conference."

I told him about George. "He's a great guy," I said.

"He is." Jesse knew him from Quantico.

"But that was the wrong job for him. He's good with tech, not people."

I felt an odd nostalgia for George and made a mental note to give him a call. I still had my own drone. Loved it. We could have fun.

"It's odd," Jesse said, "that the most important thing you did with Annan—defusing that nuclear standoff—was the *first* thing."

"On one level, it's super weird," I said. "But it didn't feel like a new relationship. Annan ritualized relationships and made people feel like he'd been waiting his whole life to meet them."

"He's still overseas?"

"Yeah, he said he'd come back often. But he hasn't." Remembering that made the butterflies in my stomach come back.

"You and Annan owe Jack Johnson on that one," Jesse said. "Cowboy Jack! Never met a mission he didn't love."

"We need more guys like him now," I said.

"Yeah, but maybe dialed *down* a little? You called in *your own lead* on that!"

"Okay, but I did it right in front of Jack. You said he had a clear pattern of that kind of thing. That's the fourth sign: actions, or patterns of positive behavior."

"Did you hear that Jack is sick?"

I hadn't. Jesse told me what it was, and it was bad.

"I'll go see him," I said. I knew that was why he'd told me.

"Sign five," I said. "I call it the language of trust, because it's derived from the Code of Trust, which you helped me create back in New York. It's listening to how somebody talks, and looking for nonjudgmental, validating statements that empower people with options. If somebody does that naturally, you can count on them."

"I love the Code," he said. "I learned a lot from it."

"*You* learned from *me*?"

"It happens. It's like the Infinite Monkey Theorem: Give a million monkeys a million typewriters for a million years, and they'll eventually write a book."

"Or in my case, three, Obi-Wan."

I told Jesse that the fifth sign was the language of trust, but I didn't mention that I'd recognized its importance from what Mr. X—the

Silicon Valley executive—*didn't* say. Not out of animosity. As Mr. X revealed more and more of himself with his language, he failed to make much of an impression on me, as a person. People you don't trust leave your life without a trace. And that's a good thing.

"Last sign," I said, "and last call." I signaled the waiter for another round of stout.

"Sign six is emotional stability. I learned that one from a woman named Susan, who helped me with a Chechen War operation. I was still trying to save the whole world all at once, and she showed me how much can be done with a quiet mind. She's in Asia now, working intelligence. Just had a baby." That seemed important to mention. I was looking forward to some pictures.

Jesse was gazing at the ceiling, lost in thought. Then he looked at me and said, "I can predict this one. Your idea of emotional stability is somebody who hates drama, doesn't enjoy power, listens well, is humble, and stays rational when everybody else is freaking out. Close enough?"

"You forgot Rule Number One," I said.

"I *do* remember! I taught you that. Rule Number One: Don't f**k yourself up!"

"Right! You said, 'Leave that to other people! They're not as good at it as you are, because everybody is their own best enemy!'"

We clinked our glasses together for the last time. Then he left. I watched him walk to his car. When I was alone, I was expecting the sick, sad feeling to return. But it didn't. I'd thought that the feeling had come from leaving my job. But it wasn't about the work. Or the money. Or the excitement. Or the sense of purpose.

My dread was letting go of the people—Leo, Annan, Jesse, Sergei, Jack, George, Susan, and so many others: the living and the lost.

But just realizing why I felt empty was enough to make it go away. That's the power of *reality*. It's usually so much kinder than the imagination. Real life, even in dark days, is never as unbearable as it is in our nightmares and daydreams.

Reality can always be altered. The vast majority of problems—stripped of the dread of worst-case scenarios—yield to teamwork, time, and logic. And memories alone can summon the lost.

You may remember from chapter 2 that in the dark days after 9/11, a girl named Emily handed me a Gatorade and a note that said, "Thank you for saving America." Back then, I'd felt nothing but shame, because I knew I couldn't live up to that sentiment. But I'd promised myself I'd save one person. That was Leo. It wasn't *enough* for me. Then. Looking back, I am in awe of all that I did not know.

Everyone who leaves a job loses people to time, distance, and eventually death. But my loss, I think, was even more poignant than the norm, because I came to my people with the mission of learning what lay within their souls. Once you look inside someone so deeply that you choose to trust them with your dreams, and accept their dreams as your own, a golden moment is born that outlives you both.

Trust lives inside that moment. When you offer to share your fate with someone through the linkage of trust—which can be even harder to offer than love—you're sealed in a bond that enriches your life as long as it lasts, even after they're gone.

They don't age, they don't change, they don't leave your heart, and you're never the same, because part of them became you. And just as surely, part of you is inside them, and may someday inhabit the lives of their children and many others—scattered in time and place, but enduring still as fragments of your life begin again.

It was still the same idle Monday afternoon, but I no longer felt empty. Immense changes lay ahead, but my fear of *loss* was gone.

The past, the present, the success, the failure, the thrill, the work, the goals—all of that fades, like old pictures. One day they grow dark, and then brittle, and soon are gone.

Everything fades but the people, and the relationships, as bonds grow golden, and life goes on.

ACKNOWLEDGMENTS

Much more than most books, this one was a team effort, and we are grateful for all the help we had.

Niki Papadopoulos, our editor, was closely involved from the very beginning until the end, and carefully crafted the book to communicate with a broad readership about the most important elements of their lives. Niki understands readers on a deep level, and is brilliant about knowing what they want, and why.

Adrian Zackheim, founder and publisher of Portfolio, backed the book when it mattered most, as just one small part of his storied career.

Nat Jacks, our masterful agent at Inkwell Management, was the guiding light of the project even before Niki, so this book is his as much as anyone's.

Publishing maestro Richard Pine, a founder and partner at Inkwell, supported, as always, everything necessary to turn a project into a book.

Rebecca Shoenthal, who works with Niki, kept a complex endeavor working smoothly and agreeably, and when she ascended in the publishing world, Chase Karpus became the ramrod.

Chassagne Shaffer and Kathie Baker worked many weeks and many weekends on a shifting variety of tasks that seemed at times to have no end.

Our families gave us the love and help that made two years of hard work into happy ones.

Our lifelong gratitude, for helping to create something that may live beyond our lives, goes to all.

Robin Dreeke and Cameron Stauth

INDEX